MW01289510

Also by the Author
The Coyote Wars

This novel is dedicated to the brave men and women of American law enforcement, who everyday put their lives on the line to keep us safe.

When embarking on a journey of revenge, first dig two graves.
—Confucius

THE LAST COYOTE

A Story of Revenge and Redemption

ONE

Rebirth

Alexa Wallace was the most hunted person on the planet. It would, however, be impossible to discern this from simple observation. She was serene and unconcerned as she looked about.

Following the terrorist attacks the week before, the FBI placed her on its Ten Most Wanted list, and a reward of $10 million dollars was placed on her head. The only other person ever meriting such a high reward was Osama Bin Laden.

Alexa's coworkers at Xion Corporation had been interviewed at length, and a sketch was created. It was displayed everywhere, including electronic billboards around the country.

As she held a copy of the *Washington Post*, Alexa smiled in amusement at the sketch on the front page. She had already cut her hair, which altered her appearance considerably. From her training at the Fortress, her family had taught her how to live as a fugitive and avoid detection. As she waited in line, she attracted no attention. She seemed like any ordinary twenty-three-year-old waiting for service.

Finally a young teller called out "Next," and Alexa moved forward. The teller had a nameplate on the counter. It read "Sally White."

"Hi, I'm Amanda Fisher," Alexa said in a friendly tone. She handed White her driver's license.

"Yes, Ms. Fisher. I remember you opened an account here yesterday. Welcome to Virginia First." The teller greeted her new customer.

"That's right. I just moved to an apartment nearby." Alexa's mind revisited her meeting with Mr. Klingman, the owner of her apartment. He had scrutinized her up and down, but smiled broadly when she flashed $4,500 in cash—first month, last month and security deposit. He quickly produced a lease, which she signed eagerly.

"Yeah, I just want to make another deposit." Alexa handed White $2,500 in twenty-dollar bills.

Alexa knew that all US banks are required to report to the US Treasury any cash transactions of $10,000 or more. These are called suspicious activity reports (SARs). The Treasury in turn notifies the FBI and IRS. Her plan was to make periodic deposits well under that limit to avoid any unwanted scrutiny. She had considered using cash exclusively, but she was worried her fugitive fund of $50,000 might be stolen. In addition, it would be useful to have a "legitimate" bank account.

White took the cash and placed it in an automatic bill counter. The bills were quickly shuffled and the counter read 125. White took the money out, and repeated the procedure. The reading was the same on the second try. She then generated a receipt, which she handed Alexa.

"Ms. Fisher, so you know, we don't need to see your ID for a deposit," White said helpfully.

"Oh, OK. Thank you," she said and walked out of the bank.

As she stepped out into the chilly Virginia air, Alexa knew full well that she did not need to show her ID. However, she was using her ID as frequently as possible in order to get comfortable in her new identity, known as a legend. If successful, this would be her rebirth.

Alexa walked briskly a mile to her new apartment in Reston, Virginia, only twenty-three miles from the nation's capital. She had yet to purchase a car. None of the many people she passed by had any clue that she was a walking $10 million lottery ticket.

———

Michael Wallace sat in his small prison cell, staring glumly at the wall. His cell had no window and nothing to distract him. In the week since his incarceration, he had lost five pounds. The food was stale tasting, and he knew any complaints would fall flat. The federal guards watching him were not about to show him any consideration. He was under arrest for a massive terrorist attack. There would be no pity for him.

Michael had already decided that he would seek a speedy trial, and he would not oppose the death penalty. The thought of spending the next fifty years like an animal in a cage was inconceivable to him. He would not allow it. He had been kept in isolation, so he was unaware of Alexa's status. Had she been captured? He wondered this and other things as he tried to fight the monotony.

He looked forward to his next scheduled meeting with his court-appointed attorney, Justin Stackmore. The attorney seemed relatively competent to Michael. He considered how Stackmore would take the news of his defense strategy. He would call it a "nondefense" approach.

His mind drifted back to Alexa. If she was still free, he knew she would be scheming. He knew how clever his favorite sibling could be.

———

Once at her apartment, Alexa sat on a small, puffy leather chair that she had purchased at a nearby yard sale. She decided that she would formulate her plans from her comfortable new chair. She opened the *Washington Post* to read the article about the terrorist attack that her family called "Coyote One."

Once the media learned that Alexa and her siblings called themselves coyotes, they couldn't let that go. The media had started referring to the attack as "the Coyote Wars," or, alternately, "the Coyote attacks." The article quoted several of her former coworkers, almost all of whom described her as "reserved" and "private." None could believe that she had anything to do with that horrible day.

The article then described the investigative team assigned the task of tracking her down. She used her index finger to scroll through the article, which she read twice. Alexa wanted to know all she could about Carlos Sullivan and his team of fugitive hunters. Her father had always trained her that one must study the enemy. A failure to do so would lead to failure. Alexa knew she had much to do. She folded the newspaper and leaned back in her chair pensively.

Now that she had lodging, her next task was to find a job. She knew that her fugitive fund had already dwindled to $43,000. It would not last forever. In her mind she already knew where she would be working. It could be no other place.

TWO

SIX MONTHS LATER

Pressure

The mid-March climate in Northern Virginia was moderate by the usual standards. The leaves appeared to be budding in the uncharacteristic warmth. Squirrels were milling about, chasing each other flirtatiously up and down the trees as if spring had finally arrived. Even the ants started emerging from their underground homes.

Carlos Sullivan watched it all unfold as he shifted uncomfortably in a small metal folding chair. He turned to the main scene: FBI employees streaming into the outdoor patio of the FBI Academy's atrium. He hated ceremonies. Next to him, as always, was Jimmy Conrad. As impossible as it seemed, the attacks appeared to have created an even stronger bond between them. Over the last months, as Conrad recovered from his injuries sustained during the terrorist attack, Sully rarely left his side.

Trish O'Keefe sat next to Conrad. A month after the incident, Conrad had proposed marriage. They were planning a wedding for the fall. As they sat waiting for the ceremony to begin, they smiled at each other as only people in love do. Sully looked over at them, pleased that things were working out for them. At the same time, it was a bitter reminder of what he had lost.

Kathy Fuller sat next to O'Keefe. Sully looked over at her as she sat fuming. She was not pleased. For reasons that eluded Sullivan's grasp, Fuller had become involved in what had become known in the FBI as the Grant dispute. After Kyle Grant's murder at the Coyote Fortress, two camps had competing views of how to honor him.

One camp at FBI HQ felt that Grant should be granted the status of an honorary FBI agent, thus granting him a place in the Hall of Honor. This was a small shrine reserved in every FBI office honoring agents who died in service to their country. Fuller was in this camp.

The competing camp felt that although they sympathized with Grant's tragic fate, he had never reported for duty, thus he never served the FBI. This group felt that it would be sufficient to place a plaque at the FBI Academy since that was where Grant was headed before he was kidnapped. This dispute went back and forth until Director Franklin sided with the second group. Franklin was now at Quantico to dedicate the memorial to Grant. Sullivan had been reluctantly talked into sending the team to the ceremony. He told the team that he had no position on the matter. Conrad had followed Sully's lead on the issue. Fuller, however, would not let it go.

As they waited for the seats to be filled, Fuller leaned forward from her chair toward Sullivan.

"I hope you are happy." She glared.

"Fuller, I had no say in this. I'm not involved." He was exasperated.

"You could have talked to the director, let him know Grant should get full honors!" she said in a high whisper.

"We have more important things to worry about. You don't know the pressure I'm under." He was starting to get a headache.

"It's important, Sully."

"He doesn't even have any family. And all his friends were killed, remember." He shot back.

"You can be such a jackass, Sully." She sat back, arms folded.

Conrad refused to get drawn into the argument. Likewise, O'Keefe quietly grabbed Conrad by the arm.

After the ceremony Director Franklin walked toward the team, but then veered off. He visibly glared at Sullivan before turning his back on them and walking out of the patio. Fuller looked at Sully, for the first time sensing what he had been dealing with.

———

Michael Wallace tapped his foot impatiently against the metal floor of the visiting room as Justin Stackmore continued talking. Wallace had practically stopped listening.

"You just can't plead guilty. It doesn't work that way," his lawyer stated for the fifth time. "We will plead guilty only if the government takes the death penalty off the table. I won't let them kill you," he said flatly.

"Mr. Stackmore," Wallace said, leaning forward to get his attention, "on April 19, 1995, Timothy McVeigh—who was also a veteran, I might add—bombed the Oklahoma City Federal Building. He killed one hundred sixty-eight people. He was executed in June of 2001."

"And?"

"To date, that is the fastest execution of modern times."

"Yes, that was horrible." Stackmore grimaced.

"Well, I want to beat that record." Wallace pointed at his lawyer for emphasis.

Stackmore put his hands to his forehead. He had never had such an intransigent client. After a moment he decided to leverage some information he had held back from his stubborn client. Perhaps it would work to change his mind. However, it could come at a cost. Judge Morgan Wheeldon, at the prosecution's request, had ordered Stackmore not to discuss with his client the status of Alexa Wallace. This had frustrated Michael to no end.

"There is something you should know," he whispered.

Wallace looked up, his eyes fixed on Stackmore. He said nothing. After a few seconds, he nodded slightly, indicating that Stackmore should speak.

"She is free, Michael. They have no idea where she is," he said quietly.

Michael leaned back slightly. He smiled. "I knew it," he said finally.

"Then all the more reason to live, Michael," he pleaded.

Michael started rocking gently on the metal bench, stroking his chin thoughtfully. Stackmore watched his client process this new information. After a minute or so, Michael spoke.

"This is great news. Death row or life in prison—I don't care. I just want to be sent to a prison as soon as possible." He grinned.

Stackmore scratched his head, puzzled.

THREE

Friends

Kathy Fuller sat quietly, alone, in the living room of her small South Boston apartment. It was a first-floor apartment in a triple decker on I Street, two blocks from the beach. Next door to her unit was the tiny *Quencher* Tavern, where locals would grab a beer after a long day at work. On warm summer nights, Fuller would open her windows and, when the breeze was just right, she could smell a combination of the hoppy draft beer and the salty ocean air. Now, however, because of the exceptionally harsh winter, the window was still closed for the season.

She reclined back against a high-back chair with the back facing her front window. Fuller had recently put the chair in that position because of a nosy neighbor and his obnoxious girlfriend who had the habit of looking in her window from across the street. She had thought of approaching them with her badge but thought the better of it. That might backfire, she feared. He and the girlfriend had the gaunt, pale look of Southie junkies, and she knew how unpredictable they could be. Best to ignore the snoops, she decided.

As she waited for her visitors, Fuller studied the living-room wall across from her. In a triangular shadow box, Fuller had placed an American flag that was flown on a US Special Forces mission in Afghanistan. She spent six months on assignment to Kabul as an FBI liaison to one of the teams during the war. The flag had been presented to her as a gift from the base commander. Next to the flag was a plaque indicating the unit that flew the flag and the date, June 8, 2005. It was one of her prized possessions.

Fuller sat patiently, stroking her cat Calisto, her large fluffy tail wagging in delight as she pet her. Finally, she heard a loud rap on her door. She knew from the sound, it was Sully. She jumped up and went to the door.

"Fuller, thanks for hosting this meeting," Sullivan said smiling.

"Listen, sorry about Quantico. I was in a bad—"

Sullivan cut her off, his hand motioning to her. "No worries."

Sullivan took a seat across from where Fuller had been sitting. Calisto watched him carefully from Fuller's chair. The cat had not decided whether she liked Sullivan or not.

Before Fuller could sit down, the door rapped again.

"Hi Kathy," O'Keefe beamed. Conrad was behind her, holding a bottle of wine.

Sullivan realized he had come empty-handed. *Crap*, he thought.

O'Keefe and Conrad embraced Fuller, and then took a seat on the couch, directly underneath her flag display.

Drinks were poured and they sat, chitchatting for about ten minutes. Sullivan was uncharacteristically quiet, so there was a slight tension in the room.

After a bit, Fuller addressed the elephant in the room.

"So, Sully, where do we stand?" she said.

"What do you mean?"

"You asked for us all to meet. What's up?" she said flatly.

Conrad felt he needed to say something as he had known Sully the longest.

"Yeah, Sully, you're not yourself lately. What gives?" He looked sternly.

Sullivan grimaced uncomfortably. He looked over at O'Keefe for support, but saw none.

"You *have* been different lately, Sully," O'Keefe jumped in.

After a moment, Sullivan looked down at the floor. He then looked up at them.

"Tomorrow will be the six-month anniversary of the attacks," he said solemnly.

They waited for him to continue.

"I'm hearing rumors that the SAC is going to take the case from us. The National News Network will be running a special tomorrow that is going to make me look like a fool. We've had no luck tracking the last coyote."

O'Keefe couldn't listen anymore. "Sully, we have tried everything."

"Maybe…not everything," Sully replied cryptically.

Conrad remembered one possibility.

"What about that new agent I told you about?" he said. "You remember, the cyber expert who wants to join the team."

"She sounds arrogant," Sully said, arching an eyebrow.

"Seriously, Sully, you are calling someone arrogant." Conrad smiled, and O'Keefe rolled her eyes.

"What's her name?" Fuller asked with curiosity.

"Suzanne Goldwein," O'Keefe chimed in.

"She claims to be a computer wizard, claims she can turn things around," Conrad added.

"No," Sullivan said with finality.

"So then what's the plan?" Conrad asked.

"Let's get the entire team together to watch the NNN special tomorrow. Maybe something will come to us," Sully said, rising from his chair.

He stood at the door before leaving. "You know I love you guys," Sullivan said, half smiling. With that, he walked out.

After he left, Conrad watched him from the window.

"I think he's got something up his sleeve," he said.

O'Keefe and Fuller hoped he was right.

—

The Reston Regional Public Library in Reston, Virginia, is one of the largest in the state. It has a simple, modern, boxy design that is not aesthetically pleasing, but it is utilitarian. It has a large collection of hardcover books and an area for the sale of used books, which receives a lot of foot traffic. There is also a section with most major US newspapers, a curious relic of times past.

In the far left corner of the first floor, there are several tables with desktop computers for Internet access. Only a few blocks from Alexa's apartment, it was the perfect staging ground for her research. Alexa had also noticed that there were no security cameras in the library.

Alexa sat at one of the tables, having logged into the free Internet connection. She had a note pad and pencil on the table next to the keyboard. For security reasons she knew that the anonymity of using a public Internet facility gave her all the protection she needed. Her Internet searches could not be traced back to her, or so she calculated.

She sat in front of her keyboard with an icy determination. Each keystroke seemed to sound harder as she pressed the letters, writing into the search engine, "Carlos Sullivan, FBI."

FOUR

Deadline

Assistant Special Agent in Charge (ASAC) Gibbons was bored and despondent. After the Coyote Wars incident, FBI HQ sent an inspection team to Boston to interview him. Central to their investigation was his poor judgment. He had taken the word of an infiltrated terrorist posing as Agent Kyle Grant, new to the job, over the veteran FBI agent Carlos Sullivan. To say that Gibbons had egg on his face was an understatement. It was more like an entire omelet splattered over him.

After the official review, Gibbons was reassigned to a position of lesser importance. In typical Bureau fashion, he was not actually demoted. He was given the title of "special events facilitator" and told to move into a smaller office. He would have no secretary. At first he started to think that he was actually given a position of some importance. However, when he approached his superior about an upcoming event he should coordinate, he was told, *Not this one, Gibbons; we will let you know.* After three such exchanges, Gibbons got the message. His superiors were hoping not to see or hear from him again. In fact, they were hoping he would retire and become just a bad memory.

In his boredom he had started taking long walks through the Boston Common. However, after being hassled by some homeless vagrants while he rested on a park bench, he decided to stay closer to his office. His new entertainment was to stand just outside his office door, watching employees come and go. Some of the female employees had started to whisper among themselves about how creepy he seemed.

On this occasion, as he stood in the hallway, he spied Sullivan walking toward him, no doubt on his way to the Command Center. Gibbons grimaced sourly at the sight of Sullivan and his cocky swagger. His every body movement and gesture seemed to mock Gibbons. Without even speaking, Sullivan seemed to taunt his former nemesis.

Gibbons stood rigidly still as Sullivan got closer. Each step Sullivan took felt like the stomping of a T. rex approaching. *Boom...Boom... Boom.* Gibbons imagined the ground shaking as Sullivan approached.

As he finally walked by, Sullivan looked over and smiled. "Have a nice day, Mr. Gibbons," he said as he strode by.

———

The Command Center was abuzz with activity. Sullivan noticed Trish O'Keefe conferring with a dozen analysts who had been assigned to her. They sat in a circle as O'Keefe held a spreadsheet in one hand.

At the far end of the room, Kathy Fuller was talking to Whitworth, the special agent in charge (SAC) of the Boston FBI. He had avoided any punishment from FBI HQ over the Grant debacle by blaming Gibbons. Next to Whitworth were two of his ASACs, Billings and Rand. The SAC had insisted on a daily briefing on the Coyote investigation as he was getting a lot of heat from Washington. When Sullivan saw this, he veered in the opposite direction. He felt Fuller was more diplomatic, so he was happy to let her handle the brass.

Sullivan then spotted Jimmy Conrad sitting in front of the large-screen TV, which he had just tuned to NNN, the twenty-four-hour cable news channel. As he adjusted the volume, Sully took a seat next to him.

Conrad looked over and smiled. Sully put a hand on his shoulder.

"Let the show begin," Sullivan said, leaning back. Everyone in the command center stopped what they were doing and started watching the program.

"Welcome to the National News Network, Special Report," the white-haired newscaster, Tom Richards, intoned. "The Coyote attacks—six months later, what have we learned? With an update on the investigation, we turn to investigative reporter Katrina Walters live at FBI HQ. Over to you Katrina..." he said with a serious demeanor.

The camera then zoomed to Walters standing outside the FBI's Hoover Building. She wore high heels with a long brown jacket that made it impossible to see her outfit. Her blond hair was pulled back in a bun. She held a microphone in her left hand.

"What we know, of course, is disturbing. The FBI was penetrated by a terrorist who assumed the identity of a new trainee. He was then posted to the Boston office, where he was able to falsely accuse the one FBI agent who appeared to be on to him. He then went on to assassinate the FBI director." She looked straight at the camera, the FBI building behind her.

"Yes, this was Agent Sullivan, correct Katrina?"

"That's right, Tom. He was placed in charge of the investigation, but as we can see, he has been completely inept in his hunt for the last coyote, Alexa Wallace."

"What do we know about her, Katrina?" Richards asked.

"Very little, according to my sources, despite the fact that she worked at a pharmaceutical firm in Delaware." Her expression radiated disapproval.

"Does the FBI have a plan, or are they incapable of catching one female fugitive?" Richards said mockingly.

Conrad put a hand on Sully's back for a moment.

"My sources tell me that the people in charge behind me here are prepared to take the investigation themselves. They are not happy with the results coming from Sullivan and his team in Boston." She pointed at the Hoover Building behind her with her thumb.

"Katrina, wasn't there some other controversy about Agent Sullivan?"

As scripted, Walters was prepared, "Yes, Tom, Agent Sullivan was involved in a double shooting in Boston about fifteen years ago. While he did receive a medal for his actions, there were rumors that something just was not right about the incident," she said gravely.

As the camera went back to Richards, Sullivan reached for the remote and turned the TV off. He stood and faced the task force. At that moment, he noticed Fuller, dismissed by the brass, start to walk toward him. As she did so, she briefly stopped at O'Keefe's station and pulled her by the arm.

"Everybody back to work," Sullivan addressed them. Most of the people nodded in assent, and the room started buzzing with commotion again.

Conrad stood next to Sullivan as Fuller approached with O'Keefe in tow.

"I have some bad news," Fuller told the group.

"How long do we have?" Sullivan said knowingly.

"Two weeks."

Conrad's face contorted angrily. "It's not right!"

"Don't worry, guys. I have a plan," Sullivan said with his trademark flair.

"You have a plan to find her?" O'Keefe's eyes widened.

"No, my plan is for her to come to us." Sullivan grinned mischievously.

———

That evening, Sullivan lay faceup in his darkened bedroom. His closed eyes moved back and forth furiously. He began twitching, and he started to sweat in his sleep. In his dream he was pointing his pistol at the head of a frightened criminal on his knees, begging. He pulled on the trigger over and over, but the gun would not shoot. Then, as he put the gun to the man's temple and tried again, he heard someone behind him.

FIVE

Federal Bureau of Prisons

Established officially in 1930, the Federal Bureau of Prisons (FBP) has over 116 penal institutions throughout the United States and is responsible for the care and custody of over two hundred thousand federal prisoners. The FBP is also responsible for overseeing all federal executions. All such executions are carried out at the lethal-injection chamber at the Federal Corrections Complex in Terre Haute, Indiana.

If Michael Wallace's intentions were to be believed, that is where he would meet his fate—dying slowly from a lethal cocktail of chemicals.

The FBP has five different security levels. Level-one facilities are reserved for nonviolent, white-collar criminals. At the other extreme is a level-five facility, especially designed for dangerous inmates who demonstrate a propensity for violence or are escape risks.

Due to the inherently dangerous nature of caring for convicted prisoners, all FBP correctional personnel undergo special training at the Federal Law Enforcement Training Center (FLETC) in Glynco, Georgia. All trainees receive instruction in inmate-control techniques, self-defense, interacting with inmates, and firearms. Corrections officers are trained in the use of a 12-gauge shotgun, 9mm pistol, and the M-16 assault rifle.

All candidates for employment at the FBP must be US citizens at least eighteen years old and have a high-school degree. All applicants are also fingerprinted and the results checked with the FBI database.

As Alexa submitted her prints, one hand at a time, into the scanner, she thought back to how she had wiped down her office carefully before escaping. She was certain they did not have her prints on file. There was also no requirement to take a polygraph examination—another obstacle that she didn't need to worry about.

Alexa Wallace, as Amanda Fisher, was one day from graduation from the latest FBP trainee class. Given her own lifelong training at the Fortress, she found the FBP instruction course to be quite rudimentary. Much like her siblings, Peter, Samantha, and Ryan, she acted like the academy was challenging.

As she walked with purpose down the hall where photos of past classes were displayed, she thought about how her family had been exactly where she now stood. She found the photos for Ryan's and Samantha's class. In both photos she could see that her siblings were photoshopped out of the picture. Alexa shook her head angrily.

—

The US judicial system worked at a snail's pace except when the system itself fell under attack, as had occurred during the Coyote Wars. In the case of Michael Wallace, his legal motions were ushered through the system with lightning speed. Over his attorney's objections, Wallace successfully filed a quick guilty plea. The only requirement was a psychiatric examination, which Michael easily aced. His sentencing hearing was still a month away, but everyone knew what it would be. The death penalty awaited Michael.

Federal inmates sentenced to death were transferred immediately to the federal penitentiary at Terre Haute, Indiana. All federal executions were carried out at that facility. However, despite his personal opposition to their involvement, Wallace's case had been taken up by the anti-death-penalty group *Humanity Reigns*. They had filed motions seeking to vacate the death sentence. Given the success rate of *Humanity Reigns*, the Federal Bureau of Prisons (FBP) decided against moving him into death row immediately.

As a result of internal deliberations on the case, the FBP reserved a cell for Wallace at their most secure facility, the Administrative Maximum Facility (ADX) Supermax Correctional Complex in Florence, Colorado. He would be transferred there in short order. In the meantime, pending his sentencing hearing, he was housed with the US Marshals Service at a secret, undisclosed Northern Virginia location. When his attorney informed him of the decision to assign him to the Supermax, he shrugged in resignation. His initial inclination was a preference for the less secure death-row prison in Indiana. Yet he knew it was now out of his hands. He had faith that his sister would get him out, regardless of where he was confined.

Michael sat serenely in his windowless cell reading *The Old Man and the Sea* under a small, tightly welded-shut dome light. He was allowed only the classics. No newspapers or current-event magazines. He put the book down for a moment and pondered his fate. He wondered if Alexa was already working her next mission. If so, he was convinced *he* was her mission. It was only a question of how far along she had come in her planning. He was certain they would soon be making history. After all, nobody had ever escaped from a Federal Supermax facility.

———

Captain Roger Sanders was a twenty-year veteran of the Federal Bureau of Prisons. Technically, he was assigned to FBP headquarters in downtown Washington, DC. However, in addition to his administrative duties, Sanders was one of the FBP's eyes and ears at the FLETC training center. His job was to monitor the progress of the FBP's trainees. He had the authority to dismiss a trainee who was not taking the training program seriously or just didn't fit the mold they were looking for. Due to the nature of the job, a corrections officer needed to have a slavish devotion to the rules and must follow the chain of command. Any deficit in this area could result in a serious security incident.

Sanders had monitored Alexa's progress with interest. He noticed that she had a military-like demeanor and attitude not usually seen in a civilian. She was a natural in all segments of her training, including firearms instruction. Her acumen in the self-defense classes had raised eyebrows, despite Alexa's attempt at appearing normal. She had grappled with larger men to a stalemate—they could not pin her down. Alexa could not help herself. Despite her petite physique, her flexibility could rival that of a ballet dancer. She was able to squeeze out of any hold placed on her by the strongest male trainee.

One time, Sanders watched her stretching and exercising after the class had already spent two hours running and wrestling. The class left for the locker room, but she stayed for more independent exercise. She could not see Sanders observing her. His eyes widened in amazement as she completed handless somersaults, both frontward and backward. All of her siblings had been stronger than her, but her flexibility and speed were her strengths. Alexa's movements were catlike.

Recent FBP policy in transferring new trainees to their new posts was simple. Graduating correction officers of the academy were posted to the closest facility to their home of record. In Alexa's case, this was Reston, Virginia. However, there are no federal penitentiaries in Northern Virginia.

Sanders called Alexa into his office after the graduation. She arrived, smiling, with her diploma in hand.

"Yes, Captain," she said eagerly.

"Amanda," he started, "normally you would be assigned to the Federal Correctional facility in Lee, Virginia."

"Is that far from Reston?" she inquired, concerned.

"Yes, a bit."

Alexa bit her lip, pondering the news.

"There is another option," he suggested.

"Yes, Captain," she said, inquiring.

"I could have you posted to headquarters, in Washington. It wouldn't be as a corrections officer, but you could start in one of our intelligence units," Sanders offered. He had been impressed with her performance. This was his way of further assessing her.

Alexa pursed her lips, quickly calculating which option maximized her plans. She quickly decided that being at FBP headquarters could allow her to make connections that would later benefit her.

"Sir, I would be honored to serve at FBP HQ." She beamed.

Captain Sanders was intrigued with this new, eager recruit.

SIX

Behavioral Profiling

Having removed themselves to a private conference room, Sullivan sat at the head, holding a folder in his left hand, labeled, **"Behavioral Analysis Unit (BAU), Wallace Family Profile."** Conrad, O'Keefe, and the ever skeptical Fuller waited in anticipation to hear what Sullivan was scheming.

"Jimmy, remember you sent the case file to the BAU in Quantico?" Sullivan started.

"Yeah, they asked for everything we had on the case. They wanted photos of the Fortress, the note they left…everything." Conrad nodded.

"Well, I've been reading their profile." Sullivan waved the folder at them.

"You told me those profilers are always full of shit," Fuller shot back.

"Not *always*." He smiled.

"Didn't you once say that was voodoo science?" Conrad added.

"I may have said that."

"You had change of heart, Sully?" O'Keefe chimed in.

"Look, I've always said that what they do is make educated guesses. *Educated* guesses," he repeated for emphasis, pointing a finger at them.

"So you think they have something?" Fuller had always been a proponent of behavioral profiling.

"Let me read a couple of key features of their report," Sullivan said, opening the file he had earmarked.

"One compelling feature of the Wallace children would be their sense of isolation from the outside world. They were fed, housed, schooled all without alien influences. The children were also given a moniker, 'the coyotes,' to further enhance their bond. This technique has been used by cults throughout history to indoctrinate its members." Sullivan looked over the folder at his team, arching his eyebrows to increase the sense of drama.

He continued, "The sense of loyalty among the children toward one another will therefore be cult-like. Any insult or slight toward the family will likely trigger intense rage in the surviving child, Alexa Wallace." Sullivan looked up again. He had their attention.

"Recommendation." Sullivan's voice rose. "Consideration should be given to use of the media in an attempt to cause the remaining fugitive, Alexa Wallace, to make a mistake or contact the investigative team, or both." Sullivan slapped the folder onto the desk.

"Interesting," Conrad said.

"I'll say," O'Keefe added.

Fuller's head nod spoke volumes.

"So we are going to call a press conference—" Sullivan said.

"I like it," Fuller interrupted.

"And by the time I'm done, she will come after me—"

"And we will be waiting." Fuller smiled.

———

The Washington Metro's new Silver Line train had a newly opened station at Reston Center. Once fully complete, it would run from downtown Washington all the way to the Dulles Airport. For now, Reston Center Station, only a few blocks from Alexa's apartment, was the end of the line.

As the train doors opened, Alexa sat on the hard plastic seat on a train bound for downtown DC. Once the train departed the station, Alexa looked out the window as a light drizzle spat at the glass. She wondered how her first day at work would turn out. She wore civilian clothes. Her FBP uniform was hanging in her closet. She would not need it as long as she worked at headquarters.

Her thoughts turned to Michael and how she would get the transfer she so desperately needed. Her first order of business was to find out where he would be transferred, a decision that had not been publicly announced. She suspected it would be the Supermax in Colorado. She knew that flatly asking to be sent to his facility was too direct. It might draw suspicion. Alexa knew she would have to be creative.

SEVEN

Provocation

The team debated where to hold their planned press conference. After some initial back and forth, ultimately they all agreed that it should be in Boston. After all, they deduced that Alexa would be monitoring their progress. She would know they were based in Boston. To hold the conference somewhere else might telegraph their trap.

The second issue was how long to lay the bait. Should the trap be set twenty-four hours from the press conference? Should it be five days? They were uncertain how far from Boston Alexa actually was. What if she was in California? Or was she in another country? The back and forth was intense, until Sullivan settled the matter.

"She is living somewhere close," he declared.

"How can you know that?" Fuller questioned.

"She will be hiding in plain sight." Sullivan seemed sure of himself.

"Is that a crystal ball under the table?" she asked.

"Moving to a rural area is too risky. People take notice of new people. They are too friendly, curious," he said.

"Go on…" Conrad jumped in.

"Here, on the East Coast, people mind their business. Nobody bothers you."

"True," O'Keefe said.

"She was last seen in Washington," Sullivan stated the obvious.

"So?" Fuller asked.

"So she is probably in the Washington metropolitan area. A lot of young professionals her age live there. It's known for its transient population. It's the perfect hiding place for her."

Fuller smiled at Sullivan broadly. "And you don't believe in profiling, huh?"

———

When Boston SAC Whitworth heard that a press conference would be called in the Coyote investigation, he immediately reached for his best suit. After all, as the head of the office, this was his job. However, when Conrad briefed him and told him the goal of the press conference was to lure the last coyote into an attempted assassination, he prudently decided to let Sullivan take the lead.

"I don't want to get in the way," Whitworth said. "Sullivan is quite capable of handling this."

———

The next morning, the team sat around their work table to finalize their press conference. A momentary silence was pierced by the sound of the wall clock ticking. Conrad looked up at the clock and frowned; it read ten o'clock.

"Well, the media has been notified. They will be upstairs at noon. We have two hours to kill," he said in frustration.

O'Keefe sat with a pencil tucked above her left ear. "Do you think this will work, Sully?" she asked.

"It's our last play," he said, placing both hands on the table.

"Have you ever used a behavioral profile in a case?" Fuller inquired.

"Not exactly."

"What does that mean?" Fuller asked.

"Well, one time, a few years ago, the BAU was profiling a guy who I had previously interrogated. I broke him, and I had the guy sign a two-page statement."

"I don't remember this story," Conrad said.

"Anyway, the guy reached a deal with the government, and he never did time. The BAU had been asked to profile him for a follow-up interview on another matter. So they had his statement—"

"Was there a problem with it?" O'Keefe interrupted.

"Well, they had scrutinized the statement. They had underlined some of the words used. They had highlighted other words and phrases. I remember an arrow or two at a particular portion of the statement," Sullivan explained.

"Yeah, that's the whole point of statement analysis, Sully," Fuller said.

"That's right. So they wanted to talk to me before they finalized their profile," he continued.

"What happened?" O'Keefe said, interested.

"Well, I had to explain to the profilers that I, not the subject, had written the statement with my own choice of words. I just got the subject to sign it. It saves a lot of time," Sullivan said.

"So they had profiled you!" O'Keefe said as they all laughed.

"They had just assumed the subject wrote the statement." Sullivan shrugged, laughing.

"So what did their profile say?" Conrad asked, chuckling.

"They seemed to think the author was an egomaniac." He smiled.

"Well, they nailed that one!" Fuller laughed, smacking the table with her hand.

"You know, Fuller, just because I'm a genius doesn't mean I'm an egomaniac." He grinned. She shook her head. "Sully, that cockiness is going to get you killed one day."

———

Before leaving the Fortress for the last time, Alexa took three weapons with her. Her favorite, as the best archer in the family, was her bow and arrow. However, she left it behind as an impractical weapon in an urban setting. Instead, she took a forty-caliber Glock 23 pistol with one hundred rounds of ammunition, a stun gun, and her father's hunting knife. It was more of a combination knife and machete. It had a curved eighteen-inch blade with jagged edges. It was big enough that the wooden handle could be held with both hands. The steel blade was razor sharp.

Alexa sat in her leather chair and held the blade in her left hand. She swung it back in forth, imagining an enemy before her. For fun, she held out a piece of paper and swung the knife, cutting the paper smoothly in two. The pieces floated gently to the floor.

With her right hand, she pointed the remote control at her new twenty-four-inch flat-screen TV She placed the knife on the coffee table in front of her as she searched for the news channel. Alexa had heard the FBI was holding a news conference on the Coyote investigation.

———

The news camera lights shone blindingly at Sullivan as he stood behind a brown wooden podium with an FBI seal emblazoned on it. Behind him were both the American and FBI flags. They hung limply in the breezeless room. About a dozen press cameras sat on their tripods, zooming on Sullivan. Just off camera, Conrad, Fuller, and O'Keefe stood against a wall, watching.

"The purpose of this press briefing is to seek the public's help in catching Alexa Wallace. I will be sharing a profile we have developed regarding this Most Wanted fugitive."

Sullivan deliberately personalized the statement so that it was from him, not just the FBI. It wasn't the FBI sharing, but *I will be sharing.*

"Alexa Wallace is a white female between twenty-two and twenty-five years old. She is without a distinctive accent. She is extremely physically fit. Alexa will routinely engage in rigorous physical exercises—perhaps even extreme workouts. She will appear aloof and will avoid making personal connections—more on that in a minute," Sullivan continued.

"Her upbringing was a secluded, isolated existence. Her parents used her and her siblings as pawns on a chessboard. There was no love among them. Therefore, Alexa will be devoid of any capacity to care for another person. She feels nothing toward her brother, for instance. She is what we would typically describe as having sociopathic tendencies combined with possible paranoid-personality disorder." Sullivan was enjoying provoking Alexa.

"Given that she grew up in a cult," he pressed on, "she will likely seek out others who might take her in. In this regard I would describe her as a stray cat, *not* a coyote.

"Be on the lookout for someone who fits this description. She is likely a new neighbor. Look around, fellow Americans. In particular I believe she is living on the Eastern Seaboard, most likely Washington, DC, or New York City." Sullivan again personalized his profile.

"No questions will be taken at this time. I will be holding a town hall meeting to further connect with the public and to keep interest alive. That will occur at the Boston Public Library in two days, this Saturday at five o'clock."

Sullivan knew his job was done. He ended with a reminder that there was a ten-million-dollar reward and the number to the FBI tip line.

His trap was set.

———

Alexa knew that any vendetta against Sullivan would take her off her mission. Yet she could not allow his insults to stand unpunished. She would strike back.

As Alexa turned off the television, she reached again for her special blade. As she practiced swinging it over her head, she was planning her next move. Fortunately, she thought, she had the weekend off from work. Saturday would prove to be a great day for one special coyote.

EIGHT

Friday

At the corner of Boylston and Dartmouth Streets, at Boston's Copley Square lies the Boston Public Library's McKim Building. Containing over twenty million items in its collection, the library is second in size only to the Library of Congress. Among its holdings are some of Shakespeare's early editions and the thirty-eight hundred volumes of John Adams's personal library. The Renaissance style structure is solid granite. It is the type of building you would seek shelter in if the city were under aerial bombardment.

It was Friday morning, and the sun shone into Conrad's squinting eyes. He was standing at the entrance, his back to the building, as he looked for observation points around the structure. He saw several, including the Trinity Church across the street. He would have at least one sniper placed there, he thought.

Conrad had already walked through the McKim reading room on the upper floor, taking notes for security reasons. Sullivan would be addressing the public in the reading room. He had already recruited fifty agents to work the event in plain clothes. Conrad wanted more agents than civilians in and around the McKim Building if their trap was to succeed. His job was to make sure that Alexa Wallace could not succeed in killing his friend. Not on his watch.

Captain Roger Sanders sat at his desk on the fifth floor of the Federal Bureau of Prison's headquarters. The office was small but efficient. He had two brown ergonomic chairs for visitors, strategically placed in front of his desk. As he spoke on the phone, he waved Alexa in and pointed to one of the chairs.

Alexa sat and listened to Sander's conversation.

"Yeah, I watched it," he said to the person on the other end of the phone.

"Sure, they had some interesting tidbits, but really Jack…that profile could fit half the city," he continued. He put one finger up, indicating to Alexa that he was almost done. She listened in amusement.

"OK, Jack. Well, let's get lunch next week," Sanders said, hanging up the phone. He turned his attention to Alexa.

"Well, Amanda, I just wanted to touch base. You've been here two weeks now." He held his hands up, inquiring.

"Yes, I really think I can make a difference here."

"Have you had a chance to start reading the BOP operations manual?"

"Yes, I finished it. Very informative, sir."

"What? Are you serious? It's an eight hundred-page manual!" He was flabbergasted.

"I completed it two days ago. Will there be a test?" she said, without smiling.

"No test, Fisher. That's quite impressive."

Alexa had not only read the manual, she had taken notes of certain key sections. She was certain her mastery of the BOP bible would be pivotal in her plans.

"Thank you, sir." She smiled.

"If there is anything we can do to make you more at home, just let me know." He leaned his head forward for emphasis.

"You were right about Betty Spicer. Actually, she is an amazing resource." Alexa nodded eagerly.

"Great," he said.

There was a small pause in their conversation. Sanders had recruited her to headquarters, and he simply wanted to check on her progress. There seemed to be little else to say, so he fell back on small talk.

"Any plans for the weekend?" he asked.

"Nah, nothing special," she said. "Just the usual routine."

She rose from her chair and again thanked Sanders before leaving. As she walked down the hall, she thought of paying Betty Spicer another visit.

———

O'Keefe and Sullivan had few opportunities to talk alone. It seemed as though either Conrad or Fuller were with them all the time. Now, Conrad was at the Boston Public Library, and Fuller was briefing the Boston brass on the final details of their plan. So they were presented with an opportunity to talk freely.

"Sully, you do realize that this bitch could easily use the Internet to find out where you live, right?" she said with concern.

"How?"

"You really are a dinosaur, Sully." She chuckled. "She could do a search through the registry of deeds, as just one example. It's easy, Sully!" O'Keefe lifted her hands up.

"Well, Conrad must have thought of that because he's assigned Agents Wheeler and Rogers to follow me everywhere. They will be at my house tonight."

"I'm just saying."

"I'm guessing she will want to make it a public murder…to make a statement," Sullivan said.

"I hope you're a good guesser," O'Keefe said, ending the conversation.

———

That Friday, after work, Alexa visited the Reston Regional Library once more. She logged onto one of the library's computers. As always she looked around, scanning for anyone who might be watching.

Once she felt secure, with her notebook on the table, she began another round of Internet searches.

NINE

Revenge

The buzz of activity inside the library reading room droned like the inside of a hornet's nest. Sullivan stood at the far end of the room, his back to a wall. A table was set in front of him, but he was alone, giving the perception that he was vulnerable. Indeed, he was. If Alexa was willing to walk in and shoot him point-blank, there was little to stop her. In order for the trap to work, there was no security at the library entrances. No searches or pat downs. In fact, Boston Police had been asked to avoid the area altogether. However, snipers watched every entrance, looking for any female matching the description of their wanted terrorist. Dozens of agents milled about, attempting to appear as civilians.

The bulk of the visitors had gotten as close to Sullivan's table as possible, hoping to hear what he had to offer. The media had been prohibited from bringing in cameras, but reporters were invited. They had secured some of the closest spots to Sullivan's table.

Conrad and Fuller stood nearby, within earshot of Sullivan and the crush of reporters. Sullivan kept in contact with his surveillance team leaders with his cell phone. From experience he knew that the use of a radio could always be detected by an experienced criminal. A person could only talk into his or her hand so long before someone took notice. Cell phones, on the other hand, are ubiquitous.

As Conrad discreetly scanned the people standing about, he wondered if Sullivan was right in thinking Alexa wanted a public execution. During Sullivan's drive to the library, Conrad lay in the backseat just to be safe. Agents Rogers and Wheeler followed from a strategic distance, watching for any surveillance of Sullivan's car. They saw none.

"If she's smart, she will come after him another day," Fuller said under her breath.

"Sullivan said she would be drawn to the media attention."

"We shall see," she whispered.

As they watched the scenario unfold, they could see that Sullivan had started holding court.

"It's only a matter of time before we find this psychopath," Sullivan said to one of the visitors.

"You seem sure of yourself," a reporter shot back.

"Not me—my team and the FBI." He nodded.

"What will you do when you catch the last coyote?" another reporter asked.

"Most likely kill her." Sullivan stared at the stunned reporter.

Everyone's jaws dropped, and a momentary silence fell on the area around Sullivan.

"Oh my God, he can't say that!" Fuller whispered loudly.

"He just did." Conrad smiled, always amused but never surprised by his friend.

"I hope he has his retirement papers filled out. The brass is going to kill him."

Alexa arrived at Boston's South Station early Saturday afternoon. She wore tight black work-out pants and sneakers with a gray top. A fleece-lined gray jacket kept her warm from the mid-March Boston wind. She had a backpack slung over her shoulder as she got off the Amtrak Acela train on track three. As she walked toward the station exit, she felt her FBP badge inside her jacket pocket.

She hailed a cab to the nearby Bean Town Car Rental company. The large iconic clock on the Boston Custom House read four o'clock, but already dark clouds had started to cast a shadow over the city.

The male clerk at the counter stood at attention when Alexa walked into the business.

"Good afternoon," the clerk said, smiling.

"Yes, I had called and made a reservation." Alexa reached for her license, handing it to the clerk.

After checking his computer screen, he found her reservation.

"Yes, I see. You need a small sedan," he said.

"That's right," she said. "A black one."

Alexa looked out the window. The wind had picked up a scattering of debris on the sidewalk. She checked her watch. She was on a tight time line.

———

Conrad checked the time on his cell phone. It read six o'clock, which they had all agreed would be the end of the scenario. It was also the most dangerous time as their target might be lying in wait. Conrad had estimated that if he were attempting the assassination, he would strike outside the building at night, when everyone thought the show was over.

Ten minutes after the crowd was told the meeting had concluded, people streamed out of the library. Some chatted at the front steps, their breaths visible from the cold air. Smatterings of people were still leaving as Sullivan himself made his way out of the building. Agent Will Streeter, an FBI sniper, peered through his scope from the Trinity Church across the street as something caught his attention.

———

Alexa skillfully navigated her rental car into a midsize parking spot within sight of her target. It had not been easy finding a spot, and she had to circle the block several times until one opened up. She turned

MICHAEL C. DE LA PENA

off her lights but left the car running in the event her surveillance was detected. Keeping one eye on her surroundings, she reached down to her backpack.

———

Conrad and Fuller walked protectively ten feet behind Sullivan as he made his way to his parked car on Boylston Street. Approximately a dozen cars ahead of them, a black Ford Escort had quickly backed into a parking spot. The lights on the car had just turned off. Agent Streeter observed a female in the driver's seat and called in to his team leader.

The driver's door of the Ford opened as Conrad's phone began to buzz on his hip. It was the surveillance team leader, Agent James Hollis. Conrad picked up on the first ring as he caught sight of the approaching target.

"Possible suspect straight ahead!" Hollis yelled into Conrad's ear.

Conrad quickly bolted past Sullivan, Fuller on his heels. As Fuller reached Sullivan, she pushed him to the ground brusquely.

Conrad had his weapon drawn as he confronted the female on the sidewalk in front of him.

"FBI. Get down!" he yelled. Two other agents appeared from nowhere and jumped on her, taking her down as she screamed.

"Please, don't hurt me!" the female pleaded.

As they turned over the pinned female, they could see that it was a petite middle-aged woman, shaking with fright.

———

From her backpack Alexa pulled out a pair of binoculars. A streetlight at the corner cast a small ring of clarity on the intersection she had under observation. Her own car was obscured in the darkness of the night. Large clouds above blocked out the full moon, which struggled without success to shine through. Alexa scanned the street with her binoculars until she zoomed in on her target. She decided she would conduct a walk-by first before determining how to get inside. From what she could see, getting inside would take considerable risk. Yet in her mind it was too late to turn back.

———

The historic city of Lynn, Massachusetts, is located on what is known to locals as the North Shore, only ten miles from downtown Boston. Among other things Lynn is known for its Fourth of July fireworks, which it celebrates on July 3 to avoid competing with the famous Boston fireworks display. Thousands of people from Lynn and surrounding communities make their way to the Lynn Beach to watch the event every year.

Trish O'Keefe was a proud lifelong resident of Lynn. She maintained her two-story home in pristine condition. The green house had a white picket fence surrounding the property, which had a small backyard. Every year she hosted a party on July 3, which Conrad, Sullivan, and Fuller always attended.

Now, the blustery March weather left few people from Lynn on the streets. Due to its location on the coast, the wind was stronger and more sustained.

As she waited to hear word on the success of the operation, O'Keefe could hear the wind shaking one of her small kitchen windows. She sat reading on her long leather couch in her living room, one eye warily glancing at her telephone, hoping it would finally ring. As she got up to use the bathroom, the phone rang.

"Conrad?" She answered on the first ring.

"Yeah," he said, "it's me."

"What's wrong?" She could tell he was upset.

"It didn't work."

"Damn it," she replied.

"Yeah, everybody's been sent home," he said, dejected.

"What are you going to do?"

"I'm going to stay with Sully in case your theory was correct, at least tonight."

"That makes sense," she said, "as long as you don't plan on moving in with him!" She tried to make him laugh.

"Ha, ha," he replied.

After hanging up, O'Keefe considered how this probably meant the case was over for the team.

———

As Fuller put the key to her door lock, she hesitated. She knew that Calisto often liked to jump at her feet when she came through the door. She decided to crack the door open and peek in. Perhaps this time she could turn the tables and surprise her cat. As she slowly opened the door, she was curious that Calisto did not appear. She walked into the dark apartment and reached for the light switch. Just as the light turned on, she heard a noise and turned around.

In a split second, Alexa thrust her long blade into Fuller's stomach as her eyes widened in disbelief. Fuller grabbed the blade with both hands, but at least six inches of it had penetrated her. She fell to her knees as Alexa stood over her, smiling, slowly pulling the blade out of her body. Alexa then wiped the blood off her knife on Fuller's back as she laid her down on the floor, gasping for air, the life slowly leaving her body.

As the blood oozed from her stomach, Alexa knelt down and watched as it pooled on the floor. Without saying a word, she took the heel of the knife and broke the glass shadow box Fuller kept on the wall. She pulled the flag out of the box and started cutting it in pieces, throwing them around Fuller's body. Fuller could not move. Her breath was becoming shallower by the second. She could do nothing as she watched in horror, Alexa drawing a coyote on the wall with her own blood.

———

Conrad sat slumped on Sullivan's couch, flipping channels on the television as Sullivan went to the kitchen to get them a couple of beers. Conrad was surprised to see that Sullivan was not as upset as he had expected at their failure. Sullivan walked into the living room, a beer in each hand. He could tell that his friend was not taking the situation well.

"Don't worry, Jimmy, we aren't done yet," he said, sitting down.

"If you say so," Conrad said, sipping his beer.

As Sullivan started to relax, he felt his phone buzzing. He looked at the screen and it read, "Fuller." He put the phone to his ear.

"What's up, Kathy?" he said.

"This must be Carlos Sullivan," Alexa said softly, menacingly, into the phone.

"Who is this?" Sullivan leaned forward. The hair on his arm came to life.

"I think you know who this is."

"What have you done with Fuller?" He raised his voice, getting up from the couch. A tight knot was forming in his stomach.

"Now maybe you can see the difference between a stray cat and a coyote," Alexa said, throwing the phone out her car window.

"Let's go!" Sullivan yelled to his friend.

—

The trip from Sullivan's house in Medford to Fuller's apartment in South Boston usually took twenty minutes, with no traffic and a heavy accelerator. Now, Sullivan was driving his Bureau car on Route 93 south, his blue lights flashing and siren blaring, determined to make it in half that time. Conrad held the strap of his seat belt as Sullivan barreled into the Tip O'Neill Tunnel at one hundred miles per hour.

In short order, they screeched to a stop in front of Fuller's apartment. The patrons at the *Quencher* Tavern looked out the window, watching as two men, guns drawn, reached Fuller's outer door.

Conrad used his shoulder to force the outer door open. Sullivan passed into the foyer and pushed Fuller's front door open. It was unlocked. He went to Fuller, kneeling over her, leaning her onto her back. Conrad went through the apartment, clearing her bedroom and kitchen quickly.

When he went back to the living room, he could see Sullivan with reddened eyes, cradling Fuller's head. Her body was still warm, but she was lifeless.

"What have I done?" Sullivan looked up at Conrad and then at the bloody painting on the wall. His voice was pleading.

Conrad didn't have the heart to tell him that Fuller's cat, Calisto, was decapitated, in the kitchen sink.

———

O'Keefe finished her book and placed it on the table next to her bed. It was getting late, and she was getting ready for bed. She usually watched the late-night news before retiring for the night, and she was searching for her remote control when she heard a noise downstairs.

Her heart started racing as she walked to the top of her staircase. In the darkness below, she sensed somebody was watching her. She reached for the light switch.

"Ah!" she screamed, jumping. "Jimmy, don't do that to me!" she scolded Conrad, who had used his key to get into her home.

When she saw his face, she walked down to him. He hugged her tightly.

"I have some horrible news," he said softly.

TEN

Fallout

The killing of an FBI agent in the line of duty is a federal offense punishable by death. Such a murder automatically triggers a massive FBI response. Given that Fuller's assassination was linked to the Coyote investigation, the response was even greater. The investigation was made a top priority by the FBI director the moment he was awoken in the middle of the night by the deputy director.

Director Franklin immediately ordered the entire Coyote investigation transferred to a new team at FBI HQ. Similarly, he wanted Fuller's homicide handled by Washington's top FBI investigator.

Conrad stood outside Fuller's apartment in the morning light, watching as Boston police put crime-scene tape on Fuller's door. It was only a matter of time, he knew, before FBI HQ sent a team of agents to take over the case. In the meantime he was talking to Boston Police detective Juan Dominguez.

Dominguez was a twenty-year veteran of the Boston Police Department and a close friend of Sullivan. Like Sullivan, Dominguez had Cuban roots although they were even deeper. Dominguez was born in Cuba, arriving in Boston when his parents fled Castro's regime when he was only eight years old. At that age his parent's put their son in Boston public schools. It wasn't long before his Spanish accent morphed into a full-blown Boston accent.

Standing almost six feet tall, Dominguez was trim and always stood straight up, proud of his accomplishments. He had jet-black hair and a prominent jaw. Dominguez had a keen street sense and a reputation for clearing homicide cases. After talking to Conrad, he was itching to work the Fuller case.

Their talk was disrupted when they noticed a convoy of SUVs drive up I Street and pull in front of Fuller's apartment. Dozens of agents spilled out of the vehicles as their leader, in the lead car, noticed them and walked over. He was middle aged and tall with graying hair thinning on the top.

"You must be Agent Conrad," he said.

"Yes, and this is Boston Detective Dominguez," Conrad offered.

They both shook hands with the FBI's new lead man.

"I'm Supervisory Special Agent Bill Walker," he introduced himself.

He looked at Dominguez first.

"Don't take this the wrong way, but this is an FBI investigation. She was one of us." He looked sternly at Dominguez.

"Understood," he answered.

Walker turned his attention to Conrad.

"The director told me to personally tell you that you are off the case," he said, pointing for emphasis.

"Also understood," Conrad said simply.

"I mean it," he stressed. "I know how you and your team work. No involvement. Zero." Walker made a circle with his fingers.

With that, Walker strode back to his waiting agents.

After he was out of earshot, Conrad leaned over to Dominguez. "Once they leave, will you look at the case?" he asked.

"You've got it," Dominguez said.

As Conrad walked to the corner where his car was parked, he shook his head as he saw the headline of the *Boston Metro News*, staring at him from the metal newspaper box.

It read, "*The Hunted becomes the Hunter: FBI Agent Killed by Coyote Fugitive.*"

When three days elapsed and Sullivan was not heard from, Conrad became concerned. He went to Sullivan's house with O'Keefe. She waited in the car while he knocked on the door and then the window. He yelled for Sullivan, whose car was in the driveway. Yet he heard nothing.

"He won't answer," he said, sitting behind the wheel.

"What are you going to do?" She put a hand on his shoulder.

"I don't know. I just don't know," he said wearily.

Justice Morgan Wheeldon looked down on Michael Wallace from his perch of authority in the federal courthouse. Wallace had not asked for any consideration when he agreed to plead guilty earlier. In front of Judge Wheeldon was the sentencing recommendation from the United States attorney for the District of Columbia. Wallace's attorney, Justin Stackmore, had given up all hope of putting up a defense. Having acquiesced to his client's wishes, he sat helplessly next to Michael. Behind them, the gallery was packed with families of the victims as well as a crush of media personalities.

Wheeldon motioned to the bailiff.

"All rise," the bailiff intoned.

Everyone in the courtroom rose to his or her feet except for Michael, dressed in an orange prison uniform. He was handcuffed in front, leg shackles binding his feet together. Security around the building and in the courtroom was at the highest level.

"*All* rise," the bailiff repeated, staring at Michael.

Michael stared straight ahead. Stackmore whispered in his ear, but he remained motionless. Justice Wheeldon waved to the bailiff, indicating it didn't matter. He banged his gavel hard against his desk.

"Mr. Wallace, before I pronounce sentence, I wish to say that your crimes are of the most heinous nature. You and your confederates are guilty of attacking the very institutions that guarantee our precious freedoms…"

Wallace continued to stare straight ahead, refusing to acknowledge the authority of the court.

"It is with regret that I cannot also sentence your remaining associate…although that day will come." Wheeldon arched his eyes.

"Mr. Wallace, pursuant to the laws of the United States of America, you are hereby sentenced to death by lethal injection, a sentence to be carried out by the Bureau of Prisons."

The sound of Wheeldon's gavel echoing through the chamber indicated that the proceeding was over. The members of the gallery nodded their approval. A legal team from *Humanity Reigns* somberly shook their heads in disgust. Michael quietly smiled. He was glad the legal drama was over.

It was now the duty of the United States Marshals Service to deliver Michael Wallace to the ADX Supermax Correctional Facility in Florence, Colorado. He was escorted out of the courtroom by a phalanx of heavily armed marshals. He had zero chance of escape on his way to his new home.

ELEVEN

Meltdown

A week had elapsed, and there was no sign of Sullivan. All calls to his number went straight to voice mail. Conrad made several trips to his home, each without success. Finally, Conrad decided to ask his friend Agent Tom Riley for help.

Agent Riley was a technically trained agent, known in the FBI simply as a "tech agent." These are agents with special skills, such as picking locks, planting covert electronic microphones, or hiding GPS tracking devices. Most of their techniques were unknown to the outside world until the publication of *Secrets of the FBI* by author Ronald Kessler. The Bureau gave this writer unprecedented access to FBI techniques that are now known to criminals and terrorists with the publication of the book. Riley was incensed when the book was released. He was furious that the FBI would grant this author access to secret FBI techniques. His concern was exacerbated because the FBI requires its own employees who want to publish—even works of fiction—to submit their work to an FBI prepublication review committee.

Riley had worked with Sullivan and Conrad on some of their prior drug cases years ago. He had planted GPS devices on some of their targets' vehicles. He had also equipped them with hidden microphones for their undercover drug meetings. Now, Conrad was asking for Riley's help getting into Sullivan's apartment.

Conrad stood behind Riley as he used his lock-picking equipment on Sullivan's door. Conrad watched the street for police since they were technically breaking and entering.

After a minute or so, Riley pushed the door open. They walked in and closed the door. Immediately, they noticed the apartment was a mess. Empty beer cans littered the floor. A half-empty bottle of whiskey was on Sullivan's coffee table. They walked through the apartment and found Sullivan lying on the floor in the hallway. Conrad rushed to his friend's side.

"He's breathing," Conrad said.

"Let's get him up." Riley grabbed him by one arm.

They could smell alcohol on Sullivan. The odor covered him like a cheap coat.

They carried Sullivan, who was starting to awaken from a drunken stupor, to the couch.

"See if there's any coffee," Conrad told Riley.

"What are you doing here?" Sullivan said softly.

"We need you back at work."

"So I can get someone else killed," he whispered.

"That wasn't your fault," Conrad said.

"Of course it was, Jimmy."

Riley was listening as he put on a pot of coffee in the kitchen.

"You need to snap out of this."

"You need to stay away, Jimmy," he said softly.

"Sully, you know I can't do that." Conrad sat across from him.

"I'm a fraud, Jimmy."

"No way, man!" Conrad pleaded, "Let's get up, we have work to do."

"Jimmy, remember the medal I got for shooting those guys in the bank?"

"Yeah, the big secret you never told me." Conrad shifted in his seat.

"I never shot the second guy. It's all a lie." He started to raise his voice.

"What happened?" Conrad looked up to see Riley listening from the kitchen.

"The guy had abused Emily Scola," Sullivan spoke quietly.

"Right. Rebecca's mom. She was the bank manager."

"Yes. I had my gun on him. I really did want to kill him. But I hesitated. He was unarmed, just kneeling there," he recounted.

"So what happened, Sully?" Conrad had always wondered what had transpired in the bank.

"Out of nowhere, Emily came from behind and grabbed my gun. I struggled, but a shot went off." He looked at Conrad.

"So you took the blame," Conrad said.

"Not the blame, the credit!" he yelled back. "They gave me a fucking medal I didn't want."

"You did it to protect Emily!" Conrad answered forcefully.

"I'm a fraud, Jimmy. Just get out...Go!" He pushed his friend in the chest.

Conrad rose and went to the door. Riley followed him out of the house. Once outside, Riley looked over, his hands in his pockets.

"Now what?" Riley asked. "It looks like he's checked out."

"Maybe there is someone who can help."

———

The next day, Conrad again pulled into Sullivan's driveway. This time, however, Rebecca Scola sat in the passenger seat. He knew that if anyone could talk sense to Sullivan, it was the daughter of the woman he had covered up for. It had been almost twenty years. He was surprised to discover that on her deathbed, Emily had told her daughter about their shared secret.

Rebecca, like her grandmother before her, was a valuable employee in the FBI. She was a slim redhead, known more than anything for her feistiness. Although she had only been at the Bureau for three years, she did not hesitate to challenge her superiors whenever she thought a rule or regulation did not make sense. Conrad thought that in many respects, she was a female version of Sullivan.

"I will wait here," Conrad said.

Without saying a word, Rebecca got out of the car and walked to the door. She rang the bell but got no response. She then started banging on the door. When that didn't work, she started kicking it.

"Sully!" she yelled. "Answer this door!"

After what seemed like an eternity, Sullivan cracked the door open.

"Rebecca," he said, "what are you doing here?"

Without saying anything, Rebecca pushed the door open and walked into his house.

"What is wrong with you?" she said, hands on her hips.

"I'm just done," he said, staring at the floor.

"Your friends need you," she said, staring at him.

"I'm just not who you think I am."

Rebecca moved forward and slapped Sullivan hard across the face. He stood, stunned, his face reddening.

"I know what you did for my mom!" she said.

He stared at her in silence.

"She would be pretty pissed that now, when the chips are down, you would give up," she continued.

"I'm not sure I have it in me anymore," he answered.

"Well, snap out of it, Sully!" She was speaking louder. "Fuller was a friend of mine, too. You need to get back to work and catch that bitch."

He was silent. She grabbed him by the shoulders.

"You need to do this for me, my mom, and my grandma. You need to do this for your friends. You need to do this for you, Sully." She spoke more softly now.

"OK." He nodded.

"Now, don't make me come back here tomorrow!" She turned around and walked to the door. She looked back at him from the threshold.

"And clean up this pigsty." She slammed the door on her way out.

Sullivan watched her from the window as she walked down the driveway.

—

SSA Bill Walker's team of FBI agents conducted a door-to-door canvass of the entire neighborhood around Fuller's apartment. Most of the neighbors were outwardly cooperative. Yet none had seen anything. It seemed odd to Walker that the murder occurred at approximately nine o'clock on a Saturday evening. There should have been people in the Southie neighborhood in a position to see something.

Their investigation determined that entry into Fuller's apartment was made from a front window. Because the window was set almost six feet above the sidewalk, Alexa must have used something to get on the window ledge. They found nothing discarded nearby that she could have used. Perhaps, Walker's team speculated, she used a folding chair or a box that she took with her. They were frustrated by a lack of witnesses.

Walker had personally interviewed Billy O'Callaghan, manager and owner of the *Quencher* Tavern, directly next door to her apartment. O'Callaghan said that Saturday night was usually his busiest time, but he saw nothing. Had Walker run an FBI indices check on O'Callaghan, he would have seen that his brother had been arrested by the FBI ten years earlier on racketeering charges. He was not fed friendly.

Similarly, as an outsider Walker was unaware of the heroin plague afflicting parts of New England and Southie in particular. Overdoses had become commonplace among the growing ranks of heroin users. For this reason Sonny Turner and his girlfriend, Tammy Smith, did not answer the door when the FBI came calling. Turner watched from a small kitchen window as the agents rang his bell and waited outside. Tammy was coming off a high, lying on their bed, groggy. After a few minutes, the feds left in frustration.

Turner's apartment was directly across the street from Fuller's place.

They still had no break in their case.

———

Fuller's funeral was attended by every single employee in the Boston FBI office. She was universally liked by anybody she ever came across.

People lined the aisles of the South Boston church as there was not enough space in the pews for everyone who wanted to pay their respects.

In the front pew sat Sullivan, Conrad, O'Keefe, and Rebecca Scola. They listened silently as Father Joseph O'Reilly, pastor of South Boston's Saint Mary's congregation, delivered a solemn sermon on forgiveness.

Sullivan crossed himself according to Catholic protocols. Yet as he fulfilled all the required rituals, he vowed to himself that he would avenge his friend's murder.

TWELVE

Colorado

Florence, Colorado, is a small town of fewer than four thousand residents, located one hundred miles south of Denver. It is most famous for the four hundred residents locked safely in their cells at the most secure prison in the United States, the Administrative Maximum Facility (ADX) Supermax.

ADX Supermax was opened in 1994 and is also known as the "Alcatraz of the Rockies." The prison was created in the aftermath of an incident at a US penitentiary in Marion, Illinois, in 1983. On October 22 of that year, two prison guards were stabbed to death by inmates in two separate incidents. The Federal Bureau of Prison's response was to create a supersecure facility to protect prison staff and the public in general as no escape was possible from such a penitentiary.

Among the rogues imprisoned at the facility are the "Unabomber," Ted Kaczynski; the shoe bomber, Richard Reid; and the Centennial Park bomber, Eric Rudolph. Prisoners are confined to their cells twenty-three hours a day. The prison is reserved for the worst of the worst.

In tier two, cell thirteen, Michael Wallace sat on his concrete stool and pondered his depressing surroundings. As he had been walked through the facility into his cell from an underground walkway, Michael could see no security deficiencies. Every corner had a camera. Everything was monitored. The steel doors were impregnable. There was a small window from his cell into the hallway so the guards could check on him periodically. Guards fed him by placing a tray through a small opening in the door.

All prisoners at the Supermax were escorted by three guards whenever they left their cells. He leaned back against the concrete wall, wondering how Alexa could ever secure his release. It now seemed impossible to him.

Alexa sat in seat twelve B, on United Airlines flight seventy-eight, from Dulles International Airport to Denver, Colorado. She had never been to Denver, but she had done her research. As she leaned her seat back, she wondered if her weekend trip would pay off. She knew it was a long shot. Yet she remembered what her coworker Betty Spicer had counseled her. Alexa thought back on the conversation.

"Asking for a transfer to a particular prison is tricky business," Spicer had said.

"Why so?" she asked innocently.

"They need a reason. Let's say you had family someplace…like in California. They might go for it."

"I see," Alexa said.

"Even better if you could claim a hardship," she offered helpfully.

Alexa pulled down the window shade to block the sunlight shining on her face. She would try and take a nap. It was a long flight.

Doctor Julius Winchester stared at his reflection in his bathroom mirror and wondered if his hangover was noticeable. He was getting ready for work, dressing in his small rented apartment in the center of Florence, Colorado. His recreation was limited to walking to the nearby *Rockies* Tavern to drink a beer or two after work. Sometimes, he would have more than he should on a work night. He was a regular, so the waitress would occasionally cut him off with a friendly word.

To say that Winchester was a bad doctor was an understatement. He had started his career at a hospital in Orlando, Florida, but he was quietly dismissed after two botched procedures resulted in a permanent coma in one patient and a needless death of another. The matter was resolved with large out-of-court settlements to keep the media at bay and protect the hospital's reputation. The discreet manner in which the incidents were handled allowed Winchester to keep his medical license.

Winchester had considered starting his own practice, but the task seemed daunting to him. He would need to rent an office, and the cost of insurance was prohibitive, especially in his case. Then he heard from a friend that the Federal Bureau of Prisons needed physicians for its more secure facilities.

In order to better contain its inmates, the Bureau of Prisons had at least one physician on call at its level-five facilities at all times. They were responsible for all routine checkups and were available if a medical emergency arose. The retirement of a physician at the Supermax presented Winchester with an opportunity he could not pass up.

Winchester worked the day shift at the Supermax's infirmary with the assistance of two on-call nurses. The FBP was not concerned with the fact that Winchester was an inept doctor. If an inmate had a medical incident, they could claim that a doctor was provided for the inmate. The quality of care for their murderous clients was of no concern.

Alexa spotted the *Long Horizons* assisted-living center as she waited at a red light. It was situated between a strip mall and a movie theater. Across the street was a small apartment complex, offering her a perfect place from which to conduct a covert surveillance of the establishment. According to her Internet searches, *Long Horizons* was one of the largest assisted-living homes in the city of Denver. It specialized in caring for people with advanced Alzheimer's and dementia.

The *Long Horizons* website was very helpful to Alexa. Under the section "*Staff,*" a photo and small bio was posted for visitors to see how friendly and welcoming the caretakers were. She noted two potential targets from her research—two male supervisors, about thirty years old. If she was lucky, one of them worked the day shift. It was a Saturday, so her chances of success were greater than on a weekday, or so she estimated.

She parked her rented blue Nissan and waited.

—

One hundred miles away, Michael stared up at the sky as he lay on a thin pad covering his concrete bunk. The only view afforded prisoners at the Supermax was directly upward. This was done so that inmates could not determine what direction was east, north, west, and south. It was one additional security measure to deter any prison-escape attempts.

From his military training and studies, Michael was well aware of the psychological damage caused by prolonged periods of isolation. Symptoms can include depression, paranoia, delusions, and often hallucinations. He knew he needed to stay mentally alert if he had any hope of assisting Alexa in his escape. He could see that the task before them was challenging to the extreme.

In order to stay sharp, Michael began performing a series of mental exercises. In one he started building a home. He purchased the land and materials. He selected a design and began construction, brick by brick. He had read that some prisoners of war had used this technique before, most notably in Vietnam.

—

At approximately a quarter to five, Alexa observed that new cars were entering the *Long Horizon's* parking lot. It was the evening shift. As she watched the employees arrive, she frowned as she noticed one of the arrivals was one of her targets, William Birch. She crossed her fingers as others started arriving.

At approximately 5:10 p.m., Alexa perked up in her seat. Dave Sutter, her remaining target, walked out of the assisted-living center and slid into a parked Honda Accord. Alexa started her rental car, positioning herself to follow the vehicle.

The first stop Sutter made was at a post office. He went inside to mail a package. Alexa waited outside, her engine running.

The second stop was at a gas station. Alexa watched as Sutter filled his tank. She then observed him go inside the station and come out with a lottery ticket in his hand.

The third stop was at *J. J. Foley's Bar and Restaurant.*

"Bingo," Alexa said out loud.

Alexa watched him park his car and go inside the establishment. She mentally rehearsed her planned approach one more time. As she did so, her mind turned to her sister Samantha. Alexa never judged Sam for sleeping with a man in order to get her position in the secret service. She knew it was justified in the name of their mission. Yet she did not think it was a line she could cross. Still, she was not beyond manipulating a man to get what she needed. With this in mind, she entered the bar.

Immediately she noticed that he was seated alone at the far side of the bar. It was early, so the business was nearly empty. Taking a seat next to him might be too bold, unless she got creative. She walked over to him with a smile.

"Excuse me; I'm not from around here," she said. "Is the food here any good?"

An hour later, Alexa was still listening to Sutter's life story. With the proper prompting, he had not stopped talking. She heard about his childhood in Colorado Springs, his schooling at the University of Colorado, and his work at the *Long Horizon's* assisted-living center.

After a while, a light bulb went on in Sutter's head. "Hey, enough about me," he said. "What brings you to Denver?"

"I've been trying to get a transfer here because of my condition," she said.

"What condition?" He sounded concerned.

"I have asthma. Horrible asthma...I get serious asthma attacks," she said, a tear welling up in her eye.

"Oh my," he said. He looked into her eyes with compassion.

"I've been told that the mountain air is good for me. It must be because the minute I got off the plane, I felt so good."

"That's true, absolutely," Sutter said.

"So I was looking for a place to live, but I don't think it matters because I can't get a transfer," she said, visibly upset.

"What do you do?"

"I work for the Federal Bureau of Prisons."

"Get out! No way, seriously?" He seemed genuinely surprised.

"Yeah," she said, pulling her badge out her jacket pocket.

"That's impressive," he said.

"It's not a big deal."

"Can't you just ask for a medical exemption or something?"

"You don't understand. If I tell them about my asthma, they will say I'm not fit for duty. I will lose my job." She was on the verge of tears.

Sutter scratched his head, thinking. "What other reason could you use?" he asked.

"I've been told I have to have a family hardship. But I'm an only child, and my parents are both dead."

"I'm sorry to hear that."

"If only one of my parents was a client of yours, I could say I wanted to move closer to my mom or something…" She let the idea hang in the air.

He fell silent for a moment, thinking.

"You know," he said finally, "you could tell them your mom is a patient at *Long Horizons*. What could it hurt?"

"What if they call and check?"

"Give them my name. I will vouch for you," he said.

"You would do that?"

"Yeah, you're in law enforcement. I respect what you do. Why not help?" he said, proud to be doing a good deed.

"Will you let me buy you dinner, once I get my transfer?" she asked, smiling.

"It's a deal."

Sutter shook her hand. She stood up and gave him a big hug.

Mission accomplished.

THIRTEEN

Persuasion

The next morning, Sullivan was working at his desk when Conrad stepped in. He looked up from a stack of polygraph reports when his friend arrived. It seemed to Conrad as if a cloud had lifted over Sullivan's head.

"Well, it's good to see you working," he said cheerfully.

"We have a lot to do. I have some ideas."

"Sully, I'm glad you are back in the saddle, but the horse is gone," he said, with a half smile.

"What do you mean?" he said, leaning back in his chair.

"You didn't get the memo?" he asked sarcastically. "They took the case, Sully. They took the team. It's over."

"I say when it's over." Sullivan seemed more serious than ever.

"So what's the plan?"

"I still have you, right?" He looked straight at his friend.

"Of course."

"And what about O'Keefe?" Sullivan smiled.

"Yes, sure." Conrad smiled back.

"Then we have a team," Sullivan said with finality.

"All right, what do we do first?" Conrad asked, sitting down.

"Didn't you tell me about that new agent who wanted to be on the team—"

"Suzanne Goldwein," Conrad interrupted.

"Yes, didn't you say she was a cyber genius?" Sullivan inquired.

"I did."

"Tell me about her."

"She was a former prosecutor. I'm told she has a brilliant legal mind. She's Jewish—not strict but observant. I'm told she can be brash. She has an interest in cyber matters. She's only been in the Bureau two years, and I know how much you like rookies," Conrad summarized, arching his eyebrows.

"Perfect. Set up a meeting." Sullivan leaned back farther, lacing his fingers behind his head.

———

Dave Sutter had just escorted one of his patients into his private bedroom at *Long Horizon's* for a nap when Tim Johnson, one of his coworkers, found him in the hallway.

"Dave," he said, "there's a call for you on line two."

Sutter walked to his office, wondering who was calling. He rarely got calls during his shift. He picked up his phone and pressed the blinking white light on his phone.

"Hello, this is Mr. Sutter."

"Mr. Sutter, this is Captain Roger Sanders of the Federal Bureau of Prisons." His voice carried a serious tone.

"Yes, how may I help you?" Sutter said knowingly.

"I have a request from one of my employees, Amanda Fisher, for a hardship transfer. I'm just verifying that her mother is a patient at the facility."

"Oh, yes," Sutter offered helpfully. "Mrs. Victoria Fisher has been a patient for some time."

"I see," he said, taking notes.

"Amanda visits when she can, but it is expensive for her to fly to Colorado, as you can imagine." Sutter had rehearsed his speech.

"I'm told Mrs. Fisher has Alzheimer's," he inquired.

"Normally, we don't discuss a patient's care," Sutter stressed, "but Amanda Fisher gave us authority in this situation. Yes, Mrs. Fisher has an advanced case."

"Thank you, Mr. Sutter, for your time," Sanders said, hanging up his phone.

After the conversation ended, Sutter gave himself a pat on the back. He had just helped a dedicated law-enforcement officer fight an uncaring bureaucracy. At least this is how he had framed the issue in his mind.

———

Alexa Wallace decided that once her transfer was approved, she would drive to her new home in Colorado. She thought the best vehicle for her needs was a pickup truck. Not only because she would blend in well with such a vehicle in Colorado but because it would allow her to transport all her accumulated belongings from Virginia to her new home out West.

She had walked around the lot of *Billy's Fairfax Used Car* Dealership in Vienna, Virginia, for two hours, taking notes. She had located two pickups that met her criteria. Both had approximately fifty thousand miles and were priced under $10,000.

Vincent Foster, a veteran salesman, approached Alexa once she started looking about for a salesman. He had been eyeing her for some time, determined to swoop in at the right moment.

"May I help you, young lady?" he asked helpfully.

"I have two pickups I would like to test-drive."

"That's great. Perhaps something more practical would be better for you, however. Can I steer to you to one of our sedans?" he said, waving his hand across the massive car lot.

Her initial impulse was to strangle him and shake him down for the car keys. *Steer me*, she thought to herself, wondering if such techniques worked on ordinary people. After shaking off her first instinct, she simply glared up at Foster.

"No," she finally answered. "I know what I want."

Her tone gave no hint of flexibility. He had been in sales long enough to know when to back off. Foster quickly surmised that his young client would be driving off the lot in a pickup truck of her own choosing.

———

Conrad had used all of his persuasive powers to convince Goldwein to meet with Sullivan. After all, he had refused to consider her for the team previously, offering her no explanation. She sat in front of Sullivan's desk, Conrad in a seat beside her, wondering why she ever agreed to a meeting.

"I'm not sure why I'm here," she said testily as Sullivan sized her up.

"When headquarters took the case back to Washington," he said without any exchange of pleasantries, "did they offer you a seat on their team?"

"No." Her answer was curt.

"But you volunteered to join their task force, correct?" He poked at her.

Goldwein felt as though she was being cross-examined. She was usually on the other end of such questioning as a former prosecutor.

"Yes, I wanted to be on the Coyote task force. However, they told me that Boston agents were not wanted." She sat, arms crossed. She resisted the urge to blame Sullivan for that.

"And what kind of cases are you working on now?"

"I'm working cyber penetration by hackers of major corporations," she answered flatly.

"Sounds exciting," Sullivan teased.

"What is your point?" She glared back at him.

"My point is this. You can join my team and make history, or you can go back to working your very boring cyber cases, protecting corporations that can absorb billions of dollars in losses."

"You don't even have a team," she countered.

"Do you believe everything you hear?"

"You are going to work this off the books?" she asked, incredulous.

"Don't worry about that. With your help we will catch this coyote."
He leaned forward.

"I don't know." She glanced over at Conrad.

"I think you should join us," Conrad chimed in.

"I'd be taking a big risk."

"The Russians have a saying, Goldwein," Sullivan said.

"What's the saying?" she asked.

Sullivan pointed a finger in the air for emphasis. "He who never
takes risks never drinks champagne."

Conrad shook his head favorably. He was happy his friend was
back.

Goldwein nodded and smiled.

———

Detective Juan Dominguez waited for the FBI to lose interest in the
South Boston neighborhood that had been the scene of Fuller's grue-
some murder. After failing to find any witnesses, the FBI task force
had decided to fall back on their forensic expertise. They were waiting
for DNA analysis of the apartment for possible clues. They would find
none. It seemed they had also given up any interest in recanvassing
Fuller's neighbors.

Dominguez, as prodded by Conrad, decided it was time to work
on the case. He considered that a visit to the *Quencher* Tavern could
be fruitful. He was not as convinced as the FBI that there were no witnesses to the crime. He waited outside the tavern at midnight, until
he noticed the last two patrons walk outside into the cold night air.
O'Callaghan was tending bar, alone, watching the final quarter of a
Celtics game. The Celtics were playing on the West Coast, so the game
was still not over.

"Mr. O'Callaghan," Dominguez said, taking a seat at the bar.

"I know who you are," he said quickly.

"That's good," Dominguez said. "Then you know I mean business."

"I don't want any trouble," O'Callaghan said defensively.

"Then there won't be trouble." He paused, staring at the owner for what seemed like an eternity.

"What do you want?"

"What did you see on the night of Agent Kathy Fuller's murder?" He glared at O'Callaghan, his eyes burning a hole in the barkeep's forehead.

"Nothing." He shifted his weight from one leg to the other.

"Bullshit!" Dominguez slapped the bar hard.

"I swear!" he pleaded as his voice cracked.

"I'm going to get inspectors in here tomorrow morning," he said loudly.

"Please don't—"

"And if that doesn't shut you down, I will be in here every night checking IDs, hassling your customers." Dominguez slapped the bar again.

"If I tell you—" O'Callaghan was starting to crack.

"Talk!" Dominguez yelled.

"OK, OK..." he said, "but you gotta promise—"

"Talk!" he yelled louder.

"The night she was murdered, I was cleaning the counter by the window," he said.

"Go on."

"The apartment across from Fuller's place, it's owned by Jody Turner," he said, putting a hand to his forehead.

"Keep talking," Dominguez ordered.

"She has a junkie son named Sonny. And he dates another junkie, a girl called Tammy Smith." O'Callaghan paused for a moment.

"OK, that's good." Dominguez started softening his tone, encouraging the barkeep to continue.

"That night, I saw a female in her early twenties talking to Sonny and Tammy," he said, hopeful Dominguez would just leave now.

"What did she look like?"

"It was dark, but she was a white girl, slender, maybe five-five."

"Is that all?" Dominguez stared at him.

"I swear that's all I know," he pleaded.

To O'Callaghan's relief, Dominguez got up and walked to the door, glancing back one last time to reassert his authority.

As Dominguez walked to his police vehicle, he contemplated how he would exert his persuasion over the two junkies who now appeared to be key witnesses.

FOURTEEN

National Security Agency (NSA)

The next morning, Sullivan sat at his desk, a copy of the *New York Times* folded in half, placed strategically in front of him. One by one, Conrad; O'Keefe; and, finally, Goldwein walked into his office and took a seat in front of him. They were all curious with regard to what Sullivan had in mind.

"Trish," he started, "tell us what kind of Internet searches you were conducting, you know, when you were in charge of all those analysts."

"Yeah, I have no analysts anymore." She sighed.

"What about our new NGI system?" Sullivan inquired.

"Next Generation Identification system?" O'Keefe spelled it out.

"Yeah, the Bureau spent millions on the system."

"Well, it does include a vast facial-recognition system, which I've looked at. However, if you recall, the only picture of Ms. Wallace was on the Metro platform. She was wearing a hat, so her eyes, eyebrows, and forehead are not visible," O'Keefe explained.

"What about the sketch?" Conrad asked.

"The facial-recognition system won't accept a sketch. It's an artist's rendering. We aren't there yet technologically."

"So what were you doing, conducting *Google* searches?" Sullivan inquired.

"*Google?*" Goldwein jumped in, "No way, Sullivan, that's amateur hour. I'm sure she was conducting deep web searches, using sites like Socialmention.com or Pipl.com." She looked at O'Keefe for validation.

"That's right." O'Keefe nodded. "Deep web searches are five hundred times more powerful than a simple search engine like *Google*."

Conrad scratched his head. His knowledge of the Internet was nil. Still, he listened with interest.

"And what did these searches come up with?" Sullivan already knew the answer to his question.

"Zero, as you well know." O'Keefe smirked.

"Why is that?" Conrad asked.

"That's because Alexa Wallace is not keeping an Internet profile," Goldwein chimed in.

"Can you elaborate please?" Sullivan asked.

"For instance, if you took a picture at a party and you tagged yourself in the photo, placing it on a social-media site, like Facebook, those deep web searches would scour the cyber world and find it," O'Keefe explained.

"Right," Goldwein added.

"So it's safe to say, this coyote is not going to take pictures of herself or put any personal information out on the Internet, correct?" Sullivan asked, looking at O'Keefe and then Goldwein.

"No coyote selfies?" Conrad joked.

They smiled in unison.

"Exactly," O'Keefe said, laughing.

"Well, what if we had a search engine that could track what people were surfing for on the Internet?" Sullivan asked.

"What do you mean?" Goldwein said, intrigued.

"What if I wanted to know, for example, who or where someone searched online for particular things?"

"Like what?" O'Keefe asked.

"Like someone searching for information on Kathy Fuller or Carlos Sullivan or Trish O'Keefe, combined with the trial of Michael Wallace." Sullivan was getting their attention.

Conrad perked up in his chair. "Is there such a thing?" he asked.

"I believe there is such a thing," Sullivan said, unfolding the newspaper for them.

"Behold the *New York Times* headline," he said, holding the paper out for them.

The headline read, "*NSA Denies New Revelations of Domestic Internet Snooping.*"

"I make it a habit of reading *the Times*," he said.

"Even if the stories are true"—Goldwein was putting on her legal hat—"the NSA is prohibited by law from sharing anything like that with law enforcement."

"That's true, Sully," O'Keefe agreed.

"Their mandate is exclusively the collection of foreign Internet or telephone traffic. They are barred from domestic collection," Goldwein stressed.

"Well, I'm calling bullshit on that," Sullivan said.

"So what do you think we should do?" Conrad jumped in.

"Can we all agree that this assassin could not have found Fuller without the use of the Internet?" he asked them.

They all nodded.

"Do we also agree that if we knew where those searches occurred, we would find the coyote?"

Again, they all nodded.

"Then the decision is simple," he said.

"What's that?" Conrad asked.

"We will ask the NSA for the information. Then we will find the coyote," he said firmly.

"Just like that?" asked Goldwein.

"Yes, just like that."

"They won't give us the data," O'Keefe objected.

"We will find a way." Sullivan leaned back. "For Fuller we will find a way."

—

The National Security Agency (NSA) was formally established in 1952 by President Harry Truman. Although exact numbers are a state secret, it is believed to be one of the largest agencies in the US government. Its budget is also a secret, but is rumored to be also one of the largest in the federal bureaucracy. The NSA is best known for its massive supercomputers that are used to crack the most sophisticated encryption systems. Much of what the NSA does was revealed in the books *The Puzzle Palace* and *The Shadow Factory*, both by author James Bamford. Given the NSA's clandestine culture, insiders privately state that NSA stands for No Such Agency.

The NSA's mission is to monitor, collect, and decode electronics signals, including cellular telephones and Internet activity. In the intelligence community, this is known as SIGINT, for *Signals Intelligence*. Its legal mandate is foreign collection, not domestic eavesdropping, although recent unauthorized disclosures by former employees have led to allegations that the NSA has exceeded its legal authority.

The NSA is headquartered on a sprawling 350-acre site in Fort Meade, Maryland. Its main building is shrouded by one-way dark glass with copper shielding to prevent outsiders from eavesdropping. It has a large two-story visitor center, which few outsiders ever see. Security clearances are required of all visitors.

Conrad and Goldwein sat on a large gray couch in the visitor center's waiting room. Having been screened by security, they had made an appointment with the NSA's director for liaison activities, Joseph Berlin. As they waited, Goldwein held in one hand an envelope that Sullivan had given her.

"What did Sully tell you to do with that envelope?" Conrad asked her.

"He said that I should open it at the end of our interview with Berlin."

"That's odd," Conrad said, adjusting in his seat.

"He's *your* friend." Goldwein smirked.

"Yes he is."

"Why didn't he come?" she asked.

"He said he was going to Colorado," Conrad said, looking around the large visitor center.

"Colorado?" she asked.

"Yeah, he said he is going to interview Michael Wallace, and he's taking Tom Riley with him."

"That should be interesting,"

At that moment, a man came out of an adjacent door and approached them. He had thinning gray hair and appeared to be approximately sixty years old. He wore a charcoal-gray double-breasted suit. A black lanyard hung around his neck that displayed his security badge.

"Good day," he said cheerfully. "I'm Joseph Berlin."

They exchanged handshakes with Berlin.

"Follow me," he said, turning and walking to a security pad next to the door he had come out of.

He placed his badge against the security pad on the wall. He then put his right hand against the pad. The fingerprint check completed, the door clicked open. They walked silently down a long corridor to a bank of elevators. They stopped on the fifth floor and walked until they found Berlin's office. He motioned for them to take a seat.

Berlin looked at Goldwein and then to Conrad, whom he judged to be the lead agent based on the simple observation that Conrad was considerably older.

"How can I help you?" he finally asked.

"Mr. Berlin," Conrad started, "we are FBI agents, as you know."

"Yes, I checked your background clearances. They are in order."

"What you may not know is that we are working on the fugitive investigation of Alexa Wallace." Conrad's demeanor was serious.

"Yes, of course, I know the case. Everyone knows the case," he said, stating the obvious.

"As you may have seen in the news, she killed our colleague Kathy Fuller." Conrad struggled for a moment to keep his emotions in check.

"I'm sorry for your loss," Berlin said. "I did read about it."

"We have concluded that the fugitive used the Internet to locate Fuller's residence," Conrad said.

"I know where you are going with this," Berlin intoned, "but the NSA does not collect Internet data in the United States, on US soil," he said flatly.

Conrad leaned his head forward and simply smirked sarcastically at Berlin.

"I know what you may have read," Berlin said, putting up his hand defensively.

"Didn't the NSA acknowledge that it did collect domestic phone records?" Goldwein jumped in.

"Only what's called metadata, not actual content," he countered.

"Mr. Berlin," Conrad pleaded, "we wouldn't ask if this was not of the greatest importance."

"Mr. Conrad"—Berlin leaned forward—"even if we had the data you're asking for, we couldn't share it with law enforcement; it's the law."

"I see."

"I'm sorry I couldn't be of more help." Berlin signaled the meeting was over.

"Mr. Berlin," Goldwein said, ripping open her envelope.

"Yes?"

"Hold on a moment," she said, fumbling awkwardly as she pulled a sheet of paper from the envelope.

She silently read the message in amazement: *"Suzanne, read the following question to Berlin exactly as worded."* She looked up at Berlin.

"Mr. Berlin, tell me again why you are unwilling to share information vital to our nation's safety," Suzanne read the question and looked straight at Berlin. As she waited several seconds for Berlin to respond, she considered how Sullivan had anticipated their failure.

Berlin's face reddened slightly, angered with the question. "I can't have law enforcement snooping into people's lives without cause." He was visibly flustered.

Conrad stared at Berlin hard.

"I have an expectation of privacy that the police will not pry into my home, my bedroom," he said angrily.

Berlin stood up. The meeting was over. "I will show you out," he said with finality.

Once outside the building, Goldwein turned to Conrad. "What do you make of that?"

"I don't know. Let's just get back to Boston," Conrad said, frustrated.

FIFTEEN

Supermax

Special Agent Jamie Banks was the senior polygraph examiner in the FBI's Denver office. Prior to working for the Bureau, Banks had served for five years as a local police officer. Banks was stocky and could be intimidating with his completely shaved head. Despite his serious appearance, he was best known among his fellow FBI polygraph examiners for being a constant prankster. This trait annoyed Sullivan to no end, especially when Sullivan was on the receiving end of his stunts. Banks would strike without warning.

On one occasion two years earlier, Banks and Sullivan were sitting together, sharing a computer during a training seminar at Quantico. At one point Sullivan was typing feverishly on the keyboard when the computer froze. Nothing he did could restore the session. Banks jumped in.

"You have an ID Ten T error," he said.

"What's that?" Sullivan asked.

"I don't know, but I've heard that's what this is."

"How do I fix it?"

"Call the IT help desk, and tell them you have an ID Ten T error," Banks said helpfully.

When Sullivan called the help desk, the voice on the other end was unsurprised.

"An ID Ten T error?" the IT specialist asked, smirking under his breath.

"Yes, can you fix it?" Sullivan was in a hurry.

"Why don't you spell that out?" the specialist asked Sullivan.

Sullivan thought for a moment. "Ah, an I-D-1-0-T error," he spelled out.

He hung up the phone as he shook his head and stared at Banks, who was laughing uncontrollably.

Sullivan was determined to return the favor one day. For now, however, he needed Banks's assistance.

Banks was typing a report on his work desk when the phone rang loudly. He could see from the caller ID the area code 617. He recognized 617 as Boston. He knew immediately who was calling.

"Sully, how are you buddy?" he answered cheerfully.

"I'm well, my friend," Sullivan said.

"What can I do for you?"

"Do you know the warden at the Supermax in Florence?"

"Yes. Warden Robert Underwood," he said. "I've had to conduct a couple of polygraphs at the facility. I've even played golf with him a couple of times."

"That's great. I'm going to need an introduction."

"You are coming here?" he asked.

"Yes."

"Is this about Fuller's murder?" he asked.

"Yes."

"All right, I will make it happen." Banks turned uncharacteristically serious.

"And, Banks," Sully said, "no jokes on this one."

Banks sighed into the receiver. "Of course, Sully, no pranks."

———

Alexa sat in front of Captain Sanders after receiving his summons. It seemed to her that whenever she was in his office, he was always on the telephone. She didn't know how he ever got anything done. As she waited for him to end one of those calls, she was already mentally mapping out her drive to Colorado. She had decided to use her new friend Dave Sutter as a natural resource in her search for an apartment as she knew little of that area. Of course, she knew that he was a loose end she would have to take care of once she was safely settled into her new home.

Just as Sanders hung up the phone, they received three visitors. One was Major James Pritchard, Sanders's superior. The other two she did not recognize, but their visitors' badges indicated they were outsiders.

"Captain Sanders," Pritchard started, "please meet FBI Supervisory Special Agent Bill Walker and his associate Agent Smith.

"Nice to meet you," Sanders said, rising and shaking their hands.

Alexa also got up from her chair.

They all exchanged handshakes.

Sanders then turned to Alexa. "Please, this is one of our new future superstars, Amanda Fisher," he said.

The two visitors then shook her hand, Pritchard shaking his head in approval.

"Nice to meet you," she said simply.

"Likewise," Walker said.

"What brings our visitors here?" Sanders asked.

"I was just showing them out," Pritchard said. "They were concerned that our new inmate at ADX Supermax might try and escape," he said, smiling.

"We have to take every precaution," Walker said.

"You must be referring to Wallace," Sanders stated.

"I assured them that no escape is possible from our Florence facility," the major said with assuredness.

During the exchange Alexa could feel a slight rise in her blood pressure. As she stood silently, she chastised herself for not remaining more detached. Yet the fear of detection was causing an uncontrollable elevation in her physiology. A slight knot was forming in her stomach. It was not a fear of the visitors as much as a fear of failure.

"We appreciate all the measures you are taking," Walker stressed.

"This is what we are good at," Pritchard declared. "You're experts at catching them—we're experts at keeping them."

They all chuckled. Amanda smiled quietly, as would be expected of a new employee. *They will leave shortly,* she thought to herself.

"Well, we won't keep you," Walker stated. Their hastily convened meeting was over.

"Nice to meet you," Sanders said as Pritchard escorted them out.

"Well, that was interesting."

"I'll say," Alexa said, taking her seat again.

"Now, back to your situation."

"Yes, Captain."

"Well, good news, Amanda," he said.

"Really?" she asked sheepishly.

"Yes, I talked to HR, and your no-cost transfer has been approved to ADX Supermax," he said, smiling.

"That's amazing," she said emotionally.

"You have a legitimate hardship, Amanda"

"I will be able to visit my mom on weekends. Thank you so much," she gushed.

"There is only one problem." He frowned.

"What's that?" Her heart sank.

"There has to be a vacancy at the facility," he explained. "They are at full staffing right now.

"Oh no."

"Yes, I'm afraid, but I'm sure eventually someone will retire or likewise seek a transfer *out* of the facility," he said hopefully.

"I understand." She got up to leave.

"I will keep you posted," he said.

As she walked down the hallway to her cubicle, she considered how to overcome this new obstacle. She realized she would have to expedite a new opening at the Florence facility.

———

Sullivan and Riley sat next to each other in the coach section of JetBlue flight 2214, direct from Boston to Denver. As FBI agents they were able to preboard the flight. FBI agents were authorized to carry their weapons onboard the aircraft. This authority was granted to FBI agents whether the agent was on duty or off duty. They needed only to check with airport security, fill out the appropriate paper work, and introduce themselves to the pilot and crew as they boarded.

Once he got as comfortable as he could in his seat, Sullivan thought back to his last discussion with his supervisor, Jonathan Waters. Although Sullivan had a reputation for butting heads with management, Waters was an exception. He was considered by agents to be "old school," and he had long ago won over Sullivan's loyalty.

"I'm supposed to tell you that you can't work the Coyote investigation," he started, standing over Sullivan's desk.

"I know."

"But I know I can't stop you." Waters crossed his arms.

"I don't want to get you in trouble," Sullivan said.

"Do you have an idea?"

"Yeah, let me take leave. I have at least thirty days of leave stored up." Sullivan looked up at him.

"I can approve that," Waters said.

"That way you aren't involved."

Waters nodded his head and turned to leave. He hesitated for a moment. "Hey, Sully," he said.

"Yeah?" Sullivan shrugged.

"Don't come back without her."

"Understood," he said as Waters walked out of his office.

Sullivan decided he would remember that conversation whenever he was dealt a setback on the case. He rested his head back in his seat, when Riley leaned over to him.

"I reviewed the list of Wallace's personal items in the prison's possession," Riley said.

"The list the prison faxed over, right?"

"Yeah."

"So what did he have on him?" Sullivan inquired.

"Well, apart from his clothes, he had a gold wedding ring, not engraved."

"Interesting." Sullivan stroked his chin.

"Also one gold Seiko watch with the words '*Congratulations Captain*' engraved on the back." Riley stared at the list.

"Even more interesting,"

"A gift?" Riley asked.

"I'm certain his father gave it to him," Sullivan surmised.

"There's also a note that he had fifty thousand in cash, which has been confiscated by Uncle Sam." Riley smiled.

"Of course," Sullivan replied. "Anything else?"

"Thirty-seven cents," Riley read from the list. "Three dimes, a nickel, and two pennies,"

"Ah, Uncle Sam was feeling generous."

They both laughed as they buckled themselves in. They were expecting a bumpy ride.

———

The drive from the Denver Airport to the Supermax in Florence took approximately two hours. Aside from introducing Riley to Banks, the three said very little on their journey through Interstate 25 south. Sullivan, from the front passenger seat, enjoyed the mountain scenery as he once again went over the plan. He and Riley had already decided on a course of action. It hinged, however, on the warden's cooperation. Once Sullivan saw the sign welcoming them to Florence, he looked over at Banks.

"What is Warden Underwood like?"

"He is outgoing and lighthearted outside of the facility," Banks replied.

"So he's different at work," Riley interjected.

"He's by the book and serious," Banks stated. "He has to be."

"I guess that makes sense," Sullivan said.

"Sully, maybe he won't go for it then." Riley leaned forward.

"Go for what?" Banks asked, concerned.

"I'm going to ask him for a favor," Sullivan said flatly.

"Oh boy, I can't wait to hear what you're scheming."

——

As an analyst assigned to the Federal Bureau of Prisons, Alexa had been given an assignment that gave her access to the personnel files of every FBP employee. The project was to review the education of FBP employees and correlate it to employee performance and disciplinary incidents. The FBP was assessing whether to require new employees to have more than a high-school diploma.

After her discussion with Sanders, she realized that what at first seemed like a setback was actually an opportunity. She started the process of reviewing the files of every employee at the Supermax facility. Instead of simply reporting for duty and being assigned a random job that might not suit her needs, she was determined to actually choose her assignment. It was simply a matter of determining which unlucky soul needed to be eliminated.

After several hours of review, Alexa picked her target. The personnel file contained everything she needed: a home address and a color photo. She then started making arrangements for another weekend trip to Colorado. On her next trip, she only had two days and much to accomplish. As she pondered what to take on this mission, she debated how much she should take from her stash of fentanyl. She knew how critical that would be to her overall plan.

——

Among the techniques used by experienced interrogators, one of the most powerful is called *reciprocity*. Its effectiveness has been incorporated into training presentations focused on the power of persuasion. It is commonly employed by negotiators and salesmen. In essence it is the concept of quid pro quo. The interrogator gives the subject something, even a small favor, and the subject now feels that he owes something back. It is for this reason that salesmen will often offer their clients a cup of coffee or some other beverage or treat. During hostage incidents, the negotiator will often send food or some other concession to obtain cooperation. The successful interrogator will likewise exploit this aspect of human nature to obtain a confession or a subject's cooperation.

Sullivan was attempting to explain this concept to Robert Underwood in the warden's office, and he was getting resistance. Banks and Riley sat next to Sullivan, listening to see if the warden could be persuaded.

"We just don't do that," he said sternly.

"Mr. Underwood, I know Banks briefed you on the importance of what we're doing,"

"Yes, but prisoners are not allowed personal property."

"It would be for a limited time."

"How limited?" Underwood asked.

"Give me sixty days," Sullivan said, not having anticipated that question.

The warden was shaking his head. He did not like breaking, or even bending, rules.

"I can vouch for Sullivan," Banks started. "He believes that this will encourage a dialogue with Wallace."

"Inmate Wallace can't possibly help your fugitive case. He has had no contact with the outside world." Underwood sat, arms folded.

"He will know how she thinks," Sullivan said.

"I don't know." Underwood scratched his chin.

"Aren't the prisoners kept in isolation?" Sullivan asked.

"Yes, they have no contact with other prisoners."

"Then what could it hurt?" Sullivan shrugged.

"True."

"Nobody will ever know. And you could be a big part of breaking a huge case." Sullivan was closing the deal.

The warden pointed at Banks. "You will owe me one."

"Fair enough," Banks said.

"What do you propose giving him?" Underwood asked.

"The watch," Riley finally spoke.

Sullivan nodded and smiled devilishly as he always did when he won an argument.

SIXTEEN

Interviews

Michael Wallace was napping in his cell when he heard a commotion at the steel door, rousing him. He was not allowed a clock in his cell, so when he awoke, he had no idea what time it was. Wallace knew it was one more technique to keep inmates off-balance. Despite the lack of a clock, he knew he had not been asleep long. He also knew it had only been two or three hours since his "recreation," which consisted of one hour in an outdoor, high-walled space, approximately twenty feet by thirty. He thus realized something else must be afoot.

"Wallace," the guard said through the door, "hands."

Wallace knew the drill. He put his hands through a small opening in the door to be handcuffed. Once his hands were restrained, the guards pulled him into the hallway, where they placed leg shackles on him. He understood that resistance was futile. If he refused to comply, a specialized cell-extraction unit would be called in to force him out of the cell. He thought it best to follow the rules in the faint hope that the guards might lower their defenses at a key moment. Of course, that hope rested on his sister's resourcefulness. In any event it might mean the difference between success and failure.

"You have a visitor," one of the guards said as three of them walked him down a corridor.

Wallace said nothing, but he was intrigued. As they walked him through the prison labyrinth, he took notice of the infirmary, where he had an intake checkup when he first arrived at the Supermax. He recalled the look of incompetence on the face of his evaluator, Doctor Winchester. Wallace hoped never to need his services in an emergency.

They finally entered a visitors' room, which was seldom used. Supermax inmates are not allowed visitors, with one exception. The rooms were used on occasions when inmates needed to consult with their attorneys. Wallace immediately recognized Sullivan sitting at the end of the table.

"Please." Sullivan motioned to the guards, indicating they should remove his handcuffs and shackles. The warden had already given his approval for that.

Once the guards had taken off his restraints, they waited and watched outside the glass room. They had a perfect view, although they could not hear inside.

"I know who you are."

"Well, that saves time then," Sullivan said.

"Time is all I have, Special Agent Carlos Sullivan," Wallace said sourly.

"I can't even begin to imagine."

"I know what you're trying to do. Do you think showing me empathy will get you anything?" Wallace asked sarcastically.

"I'm just engaging in a conversation. Do you want me to leave?"

Sullivan calculated that Wallace was too curious and bored to wish an end to their meeting.

"I have nothing else to do. What is it you want?"

"I just want to start a dialogue."

"No, you want information to capture my sister." Wallace stared hard.

"You didn't hear? No, Mr. Wallace, your sister has been captured." Sullivan stared back.

Wallace felt like he had been punched in the gut. He did his best to conceal any hint of emotion.

"I don't believe you," he shot back.

"It doesn't matter, really. That's not why I came."

"Why did you come then?" Wallace asked.

"I'm doing a research project on terrorism. I'm interviewing people convicted of terrorist acts. You are on the top of my list." Sullivan had his hands, palms down, on the table in front of him.

"I'm not a terrorist."

"Ah, how would you describe yourself?"

"I'm a revolutionary. I'm trying to change a corrupt system that you are a part of." Wallace's eyes lit up passionately.

"See, that's what I'm interested in. Your motivations, ideas, and so forth."

"I'm not inclined to help you, Mr. Sullivan."

"What if we traded?" Sullivan asked.

"What do you propose?"

"I can arrange for you to get writing materials so you can write down your motivations. Whatever you think is important. When the time is right, I can even arrange for you to send a letter to your sister."

Wallace sat motionless, pondering his decision. He was in no mood to cooperate with the FBI. He also felt that Sullivan was lying about his sister. Still, what if it were true, he thought.

"That's it?" Wallace was fishing for more privileges.

"I also have something of yours. I've arranged for you to keep a personal item." Sullivan pulled the watch from an envelope Riley had placed it in for him.

Wallace's eyes visibly widened.

"My watch," he said, shifting anxiously in his seat.

"Yes, I'm guessing it was a gift to you."

"Nice try."

"Well, what do you say?" Sullivan teased Wallace, holding the watch up for him to see.

"The guards will take it from me two seconds after you leave."

"No, I got special permission from the warden."

Wallace considered the proposal. Although the idea of collaboration with the FBI was repulsive to him, he thought it might be in his best interests. First of all, it allowed him some real mental recreation. Second, an occasional interview with the FBI was more stimulation than he was getting in his cell. He might also be able to glean information from the interactions. Besides, he knew he would not give any information that could be used against his sister. After a minute he finally answered.

"If you fulfill your end, then I will talk with you."

Sullivan handed the watch to Wallace, who quickly put it on his left wrist.

"By the way, Agent Sullivan, that was some stunt you pulled on the GW Bridge."

"I was just going to tell you the same thing."

Sullivan stood up to leave and called for the guards as Wallace checked out his watch.

"We will meet again soon."

Sullivan's final words echoed in the small room.

———

Detective Dominguez waited in his cruiser, watching Jody Turner's apartment patiently from across the street. He had conducted periodic drive-bys and had not seen anything to indicate that somebody was home. He had obtained Turner's booking photo from a previous shoplifting arrest. Aside from that one incident, Turner had no interaction with law enforcement.

Just as he was about to give up, he saw Turner walking down the street toward her apartment. Dominguez got out of his cruiser, determined to head her off. He reached her as she got to her front stoop.

"Ms. Turner," he said, displaying his badge.

Turner didn't need to see the badge to know he was a police officer. Despite wearing plain clothes, Dominguez screamed cop. His demeanor and style gave him away.

"How can I help you?" she asked, clutching a shopping bag in one hand and her house keys in the other.

"I'm looking for your son, Sonny."

"I haven't seen him in a few days."

"What about his girlfriend, Tammy?" he asked.

"Same." She looked at her door, trying to end the questioning.

"It's important that I talk to them." Dominguez was serious.

"Is he in trouble again?" She frowned.

"No, I just need to talk to him, not arrest him."

"Well, he's had a drug habit." She was getting emotional.

"I know."

"I would give you his cell-phone number, but his service was cut off."

"What about Tammy's?"

"I don't even know her number."

"Do you get along with her?" he asked.

"Not at all, Detective. She is bad news."

"Will you call me when you see them?" He held out his card.

"You know"—she hesitated—"she scores drugs for him. She's a prostitute. I can't stand her in my house."

"I can help with that."

"Then, yes, I will call you." She nodded.

She put his card in her pocket and walked the steps up to her door. Dominguez waited until she was inside before walking back to his cruiser.

———

Sullivan and Riley found two empty seats at gate fifteen, terminal B, at Denver's International Airport. They had already checked in with the gate agent, and waited to preboard their flight to Boston. Their drive back to Denver had been uneventful with Banks at the wheel. To their surprise he had actually fulfilled his pledge to avoid any pranks or antics. Perhaps it was the gravity of their mission that kept Banks in check.

"Banks really came through for us," Riley said.

"Yes, he did."

"So what's next?" Riley asked.

"Riley, you've already done too much. I want to thank you, but I can't ask you for more."

"No way, Sully," he said. "I'm all in now."

"All right." Sullivan smiled. "That's good to know."

"So what's next?"

"Once we get back to Boston, we will regroup with the team."

"How did it go at the NSA?"

"Actually," Sullivan said, "Conrad said it didn't go well."

"That sucks," Riley said, shifting in his seat.

"I expected that."

"So the NSA thing is a dead end?"

"Not at all, Riley," he explained. "That was only our opening move."

At that moment, the gate agent waved over to them. She was calling them to preboard before making her standard public-address announcement.

They handed her their boarding passes and walked onto the plane.

———

Supervisory Special Agent (SSA) Jonathan Waters sat with his feet on his desk, reviewing some of the performance appraisals he had written for the agents on his squad. They were only his first draft. Sullivan's folder was at the bottom. Given everything that had transpired, that appraisal would take a little more massaging. Sullivan had hatched a plot that backfired and led to the death of Agent Fuller. He knew it could not have been foreseen, except by the armchair agents working at FBI HQ.

As he flipped from one report to another, his desk phone rang loudly. Waters had the habit of keeping the volume high because he wanted to hear it ring when he was in the hallway. He could see area code 202 flashing on the phone's screen. Immediately, he knew it was FBI HQ. He wondered which desk jockey was calling him as he picked up the receiver.

"Waters here," he said.

"This is SSA Bill Walker."

"How can I help you?" Waters braced himself for some bad news.

"You are Agent Sullivan's supervisor, correct?" Walker's tone was pointed.

"That's right."

"I have it on good authority that Sullivan is still meddling in the Fuller and Coyote investigations, despite being warned to stand down."

"How so?" Waters said.

"He interviewed inmate Michael Wallace at the Supermax in Colorado."

"I'm sure he had his reasons."

"Are you agents in Boston deaf *and* dumb?" Walker snapped.

"How are you coming along on the Fuller case?" Waters asked sarcastically.

"That's irrelevant."

"How do I know your information is even accurate?" Waters stalled, knowing full well it must be true.

"I received a call from ASAC Gibbons in Boston. Apparently, your Agent Sullivan has gone rogue," he said sternly.

"You mean former ASAC Gibbons. I understand he has a new job," Waters jabbed.

"Whatever."

"Well, Agent Sullivan is on annual leave. I have no idea what he does on his free time."

Waters was glad Sullivan had the foresight to take leave. It was proving to be quite useful in this dispute.

"Then he has no business conducting an interview!" His voice rose.

"You may not be aware, since you work at HQ, but just because an agent is on leave doesn't mean he stops being an agent."

"Listen to me, Waters. You need to leash your agent before you get jammed up!"

"Is that all?" Waters was losing his patience.

"No. My next call is to the Office of Professional Responsibility."

"Do what you have to do." Waters slammed the phone on his caller.

With his feet still propped up on his desk, Waters realized he needed to warn Sullivan. He was pretty sure Sullivan would be unfazed, however. OPR inquiries typically take months to adjudicate. By then, Sullivan would either have succeeded in capturing the last fugitive, or he would be submitting his retirement papers.

SEVENTEEN

Operation Rocky Mountain

Given everything she needed to accomplish in one weekend, Alexa jumped on a flight to Denver on Friday, right after work. Her flight landed at midnight Denver time. Dave Sutter had received word of her planned trip with excitement. He had come to believe that they had real chemistry. They were talking by phone practically every night. He offered to let her stay at his place, telling her that he would sleep on the couch. She could have his bed. She refused politely. In practical terms his offer was a good one. She could save money on a hotel. However, given what she had in mind, it was best if she was seen on his property as little as possible. Ideally, she would only see his apartment one time if everything went as planned.

She told him that her plan was to drive to Colorado Springs on Saturday morning and check out possible apartments. She had reviewed a couple of prospects online. She would meet him for dinner on Saturday night.

He offered to pick her up at the airport, but she said it made no sense. She needed to rent a car anyway.

After she had checked into the Holiday Inn's Denver Airport location, she used the hotel phone to call him as she had promised.

"Hey there," he said.

"I made it," she answered quietly.

"You must be exhausted."

"Absolutely."

"Are we still on for tomorrow?

"Yes, I will call you when I get back to the hotel. I will want to settle down before we meet," she said.

"All right then."

She hung up the phone and started to unpack. She placed her clothes in the hotel dresser drawer. From her bag she retrieved a small bag of pills. Before leaving Xion Pharmaceutical, she had taken with her almost one kilo of fentanyl. She had used the fictional corporation her father had created, the *Benton County Veterinary and Relief Corporation*, to obtain and hide her illicit-drug stash.

For Operation Coyote One, her father had needed her supply of carfentanyl for his deadly toxin, but that was too powerful for her current needs. The small amount of fentanyl needed for this trip she kept in a double-sealed bag that she put in her backpack. She took the extra precaution of checking the bag, rather than carrying it on, to avoid the TSA bag-screening process.

The last item she retrieved from her bag was her stun gun. Checking to make sure it was fully operational, she put it in her backpack.

Alexa lay in bed and stared at the ceiling. She went over in her mind her task ahead before falling into a deep sleep.

———

Alexa always preferred to awake by natural light, rather than by alarm clock. She had intentionally left the shades pulled up in her room. The morning light, as she intended, woke her gradually from her profound sleep. She lifted her head slowly and looked at the digital hotel clock. It was 6:12 a.m. By the clock, she had slept five hours. By her biological clock, she had actually only slept three. The time-zone effect with the higher altitude of Denver had combined to tire her more than she had anticipated. She willed herself up and into the shower.

Alexa drove her rented Ford Taurus south on Interstate 25. She soon saw a green highway sign that read, "*Colorado Springs 60 Miles.*" She drove with purpose, careful to exceed the speed limit by no more than seven miles per hour. She could ill afford law-enforcement attention.

———

Wesley Hughes awoke to the sound of his black Labrador, Tucker, grumbling next to his bed. It was already seven, and Tucker wanted to relieve himself. A resident of Florence, Colorado, Hughes worked the morning shift at the ADX Supermax, from seven to three. The prison was less than ten minutes away, so he usually awoke no earlier than six. However, he had this Saturday off. It was an opportunity to sleep in. As he shifted in his bed from Tucker's commotion, he realized it was pointless. He knew Tucker would not relent until he was let out. He realized that he also had to relieve himself. Friday evening at the local tavern is two-for-one pitcher night, so he was groggy from a night of beers with his friends. There was not much to do in Florence. This was a Friday-night ritual. He got up slowly.

His small apartment was one of six units, two per floor, of a three-story complex. He had a ground-floor unit that had a small garden accessible from a sliding door off the kitchen. Tucker went out while Hughes prepared himself a cup of coffee.

Hughes plopped himself down on his small living-room couch. He put his feet on his coffee table and grabbed the remote control. He looked out the window, thinking to himself that he had another boring Saturday to look forward to.

———

Colorado Springs, with a population of almost a half-million residents, is the second-largest city in Colorado. Situated at the base of the Southern Rockies Pike's Peak, which rises to over eight thousand feet, it has been photographed countless times. It is well known as a hub for the defense industry, which is the area's largest employer. It is home to the US Air Force Academy as well as Fort Carson and Peterson Air Force Base, which headquarters the Air Force Space Command.

Tourism is central to the local economy. Visitors enjoy touring the US Olympic Training Center, among other attractions. The city is also the headquarters of the US Olympic Committee.

Alexa saw the sign to the Olympic Training Center and wondered how she would fare in the archery competition, her true passion. She resigned herself to never knowing.

After careful study Alexa had decided that Colorado Springs would be her new temporary home. Residing in Florence was not an option. There were too many Bureau of Prisons employees residing in the town of Florence. She would bump into her coworkers constantly. She wanted minimal interaction with her coworkers outside of the facility. Alexa would rather drive the forty miles from Colorado Springs to Florence each day than deal with the risks of such close association with her colleagues.

Alexa pulled into the parking lot of the *Fountainhead* apartment complex with easy access to Interstate 25. She spied the entrance to the first-floor office and walked in. One desk was empty. Behind the other was a woman in her forties with a white blouse under a tan suit.

"May I help you?" she asked helpfully.

"Yes, I'm relocating to the area." Alexa had the air of someone in a hurry.

"May I ask when?"

"Within the next thirty days."

"I see." She looked down at a ledger.

"We have two units ready for immediate occupancy."

"Excellent," Alexa said. "Can I check them out?"

After conducting an inspection of both units, Alexa decided on the unit facing the front of the complex. It afforded her a view of the parking lot and the street, from which she could check for any possible surveillance or police presence.

"I'll take it," she declared.

———

The Colorado air in April had a misty feel. Clouds were scattered in the low atmosphere, partially concealing the early afternoon spring sunshine. Despite her superior physical conditioning, Alexa occasionally felt herself take an extra breath due to the altitude and her fatigue.

After arriving at Florence, the first thing she did was locate Hughes's apartment. She made a mental note of the entryway and drove around the block, looking for a place to park when the time was right. She could not park anywhere too close. She also knew to strike after dark, yet not too late. Alexa considered that Hughes was sure to go out at some point—a thirty-year-old male would not stay at home on a Saturday night. So she drove into town, learning the roads and checking the points of entry and egress from Florence.

Alexa drove to the ADX Supermax, pulling over once she saw the facility in the distance. The roadway to the facility was a mile long up to a high plateau. From her vantage point, she could see the perimeter towers. From her review of the personnel file, she knew that Hughes was a "perimeter man." He usually manned one of the towers and took turns patrolling the perimeter. His other duty included working the intake sally port where inmates were received into the facility. On rare occasions the sally ports were used when inmates left the facility as a result of a court appearance or transfer to another prison. The Supermax had specialized secure transport vans for those needs.

Alexa took one last look up the road to her prize. It was hers if she could steel herself for the task ahead.

—

Hughes sat on his couch, alternately sipping on a cup of coffee and changing channels with his television remote. It was a habit that had cost him more than one girlfriend. One in particular, Wendy, complained to no end that he was making her dizzy changing channels. Hughes was unmoved. It was his house, and he would do as he pleased. At his feet Tucker dozed quietly.

He looked at his watch. It read 5:05 p.m. The sun was starting its slow descent behind a nearby mountain. He looked outside and observed the darkness closing in.

Hughes had plans to meet friends from work at their usual hang-out. He had an hour to shower and change into something decent. Perhaps, he thought, Wendy would be there. More than once after their breakup, he had talked her into spending the night at his place. He got up to get ready.

From his bedroom, over the sound of the television, he suddenly heard Tucker growling. He knew this to mean he had a visitor. Tucker was territorial. In a moment he heard his doorbell. Tucker walked to the door and opened it without looking through the peephole as there was little crime in Florence.

Hughes was surprised to see an unknown female, attractive, in her twenties. He quickly thought to himself that perhaps this would be a good night.

"Hello," he said. "How can I help you?"

"Yeah," she said, smiling, "I'm looking for the Wilson family."

Immediately she noticed the dog at Hughes's side. It was a detail not found in his file. The dog simmered down once he saw she posed no threat. Yet he watched her carefully.

"I think you have the wrong residence."

She pulled out a piece of paper with an address on the other side of town.

"Is this it?" she handed him the paper.

"No, you are *way* off." He laughed.

"Would you mind if I use your bathroom? I just drove from Denver, and there are no public restrooms around here."

Her innocent pleading caught his attention. *How could I say no?* he thought.

"Sure," he said. "It's down at the end of the corridor."

Alexa walked in, scanned the surroundings, and headed for the bathroom. She saw nobody else in the apartment. She saw no weapons in plain sight.

While he waited for his guest to finish in the bathroom, Hughes had the fleeting notion of asking her to join him for a drink with his friends. It was unusual to see an outsider in Florence. She would be quite a prize to show his friends.

After a minute or so, he heard the flush of the toilet followed by the sound of running water. The door opened, and Alexa bounced out of the room, smiling.

"Well, I was thinking," Hughes said, sheepishly looking down at the floor.

The moment gave Alexa her opportunity. In one quick motion, she reached into her jacket and thrust her charged stun gun into his stomach. He convulsed in agony, crumpling to the floor. In an instant, Tucker charged Alexa, grabbing her left leg in his jaws.

She tried pulling away, but Tucker dug deeper, growling and shaking his body violently. She tried using her stun gun on the dog, but he kept pulling her down as if trying to drag her out of the apartment. Every time she reached down, he pulled her again, gnawing on her ankle. Finally, on her back, Alexa used her right foot, kicking Tucker in the face. He let go for a moment, and she stunned him in the neck as he lunged at her again.

Tucker shook madly, dropped on his stomach, and lost consciousness. Alexa took his body and dragged it into the garden, closing the sliding door. As much as she wanted to gut the dog, she knew it did not suit her plans. Soon enough, the dog would awake, and he would not display any signs of foul play. Hughes's death had to appear accidental.

Alexa quickly went to the window and closed the curtains for privacy. The adrenalin surge she was experiencing masked the pain of Tucker's bite. She then returned to Hughes, who was starting to wake up. Using two plastic ties she brought with her, she quickly restrained Hughes by the wrists. She was careful not to tighten them too much, lest they leave marks. She pulled him up and sat him in a plastic chair she retrieved from the kitchen.

Hughes started to come out of his shock. He tried getting his bearings by staring at his television, trying to focus. Behind him he could hear his attacker in the kitchen. He could hear the clink of a glass on the kitchen counter and then the sound of pouring water. For a moment he thought he was dreaming.

Alexa retrieved one of the fentanyl pills she had taken for the mission. She stood before Hughes. He was confused by what had happened. *Why?* he wondered.

"I need you to take this pill." She stared at him hard.

He shook his head.

"If you don't, I will shock you again," she warned.

"Please don't!" he begged.

"I promise nothing will happen to you. You will sleep for a while—that's all." She tried reassuring him.

"Do you promise?" He was shaking.

"Yes, I swear."

"All right," he said, "give it to me."

After he swallowed the pill, she gave him some water to wash it down. Alexa then pulled up another chair and sat in front of him. She then retrieved a pen and paper from her pocket. His confusion grew as he started to feel woozy. A warm feeling started to come over him. Dread permeated every pore of his body as a helpless feeling overwhelmed his weakening senses.

"One more thing," Alexa asked him, pen in hand. She jotted the exact time in her notes.

"What?" His head started drooping.

"How much do you weigh?"

———

After Hughes lost consciousness, Alexa went to the bathroom and found a first-aid kit under the sink. She cleansed her leg wound with some alcohol swabs and bandaged the injured area. She then took the kit and placed it in her backpack. Donning a pair of black gloves, she started the process of cleaning the entire apartment, wiping down all the surfaces she might have touched. As she did this, she heard Hughes making some noises. She quickly observed that he had started convulsing, froth coming out of his mouth. She checked the time. "*Fifteen minutes,*" she jotted down on her sheet.

Alexa looked out to the garden and noticed Tucker starting to regain his senses. He was groggy, but she knew it would not be long before the dog started barking. She opened the sliding door, stepped outside, and jolted Tucker again to buy herself more time.

Ten minutes later Alexa, who had been monitoring Hughes, felt that his pulse was gone. He had expired. Again, she made a notation in her log. She then pulled up his shirt, looking for any burn mark from the stun gun. She found none.

Alexa untied Hughes and laid him on the floor next to the seat where he had died. She placed him in such a way that it appeared he had fallen asleep and fallen. She put the plastic ties in her backpack and again scanned the residence for any sign she had been there.

Once she was satisfied all was safe, she used the peephole in the front door to make sure nobody was outside. She then left his apartment, walking briskly, despite the pain to her leg, to her waiting car. Alexa knew her night was far from over.

———

Sutter looked at the clock on his wall with concern. It was almost eight and he had not heard from Amanda. He was looking forward to seeing her. Beyond that he was starving. He usually dined no later than seven. He had baked lasagna, which he was keeping warm in his oven. He paced his living room impatiently. Finally, his phone rang.

"Amanda?"

"Yeah, I'm back," she said.

"You still want to meet, yes?" he asked.

"Yes, of course, what's the plan?"

"Well, I had mentioned that I'm a great cook." He reminded her of one of their conversations.

"I thought you were kidding."

"Nope."

"So you want me to come to your house?"

"Just for dinner, Amanda, of course," he reassured her.

"All right." She smiled into the phone. "I'm on my way."

Alexa considered how this arrangement was perfect for what she had planned. Per her training, she ran over the details of what lay ahead in her mind as she pulled out of the hotel parking lot. She was tired. Perhaps, she hoped, her last mission of the day would not take all night. She had a long flight back to Washington in the morning.

———

When Hughes's neighbors heard Tucker barking uncontrollably, two of them called the police. Tucker was known to bark only when provoked or, on the rare occasion, when an unknown person walked by. Patrolman Jones was dispatched to drive by and check on the complaint. Conducting a wellness check, the patrolman walked through the unlocked door into the apartment after knocking for several minutes. Jones practically stumbled over Hughes's body. Once he realized there was a dead man in the room, he quickly radioed for the chief.

Now Chief Wayne LaPierre of the Florence Police Department stood over the body of Wesley Hughes with the somber look of someone who would soon be delivering bad news. Florence was a small community, and Hughes was known as a good corrections officer. He dreaded making the visit to Hughes's family in Denver. LaPierre looked over at Captain Richard Frye, one of his most trusted officers.

"What do you think?"

"It could be an overdose. I don't see any evidence of foul play," Frye stated.

"Can you explain why the dog was outside when he was found?" LaPierre was suspicious.

"Who can say? Maybe he was doing his business when Hughes passed out."

"I heard he was a good officer," the chief said quietly.

"We will get a toxicology report. Maybe he got hooked on drugs."

"Let's loop the state police in on this. We don't have as much homicide experience." The chief knew to cover all his bases.

"We don't know it's a homicide, Chief," Frye said flatly.

"We should assume it is until proven otherwise."

"All right, Chief. I'll get on that,"

"I will give Warden Underwood a call," LaPierre said, a sad expression on his face.

"He lost a good officer today."

———

Sutter poured Alexa a glass of Chilean merlot as they sat at his dining-room table. A small radio played some light jazz in the background. She took a sip of the wine and smiled. Although she was not a wine drinker, she actually liked the sweet blend he had selected. She had decided to enjoy the wine and baked lasagna Sutter had cooked before getting down to business.

"Tell me about your day," he asked.

"Well, I got an apartment in Colorado Springs."

"Fantastic. Where is it?"

"It's called the Fountainhead, and it's just off Route 25. It's perfect." She smiled.

"That's great."

They ate their meal while Alexa looked at the clock on Sutter's kitchen wall. It seemed to be moving counterclockwise to her. It was already nine, and she was tired. Her flight was scheduled for ten the next morning. She needed to wrap things up.

"Do you have any plans for tomorrow?" she asked more out of boredom than interest.

"I'm having brunch with my parents."

"That's nice."

"It's something we do once a month."

"What do they do?" She took another sip of wine.

"They are high-school teachers. Dad teaches math. Mom teaches chemistry." He was animated.

"That's sweet."

"They're really hoping to meet you once your move is complete." He smiled.

"What?" Alexa was flattened.

"I told them about you. I hope that's OK," he said, concerned.

"What did you tell them?" Her voice rose slightly.

"I told them you worked at the Bureau of Prisons, that you are smart and funny, and you were moving here." He arched his eyebrows, hoping she was not upset.

Alexa composed herself as best she could. She had not factored this development into her plans.

"No, Dave, that's great. I look forward to meeting them." She shifted slightly.

They made small talk for the next thirty minutes until Alexa excused herself for the night. Sutter was disappointed in the short meeting but understood her time was limited. She allowed him a slight kiss on the cheek before departing. As Alexa walked down the walkway toward the building's parking lot, Sutter watched her from his window. At that moment he had no idea how lucky he had been.

EIGHTEEN

Reminiscences

The *Kelly Tavern* was a lively Irish bar two blocks from the Boston FBI office at Government Center. The interior was an exact reproduction of a bar in Kelly, Ireland. The centerpiece was a rectangular bar with large columns at each corner. The team had decided it was a perfect venue for a lunchtime meeting. They needed to regroup and refocus.

Sullivan sat at the head of a corner table, looking about for any possible eavesdroppers. He saw none.

Conrad and O'Keefe sat on one side of the table; Goldwein and Riley sat on the other.

"First of all, I want to thank Riley for joining the team, as much as I warned him against it." Sullivan sat, arms folded.

"He was a lot of help on our Colorado trip."

Riley bowed his head with a smile. "I'm happy to help. Kathy was a friend."

O'Keefe sat silently, a small tear forming at the corner of her left eye.

"I still can't believe she's gone." She said softly,

"If she were here, she would have something funny to say," Sullivan stated.

Conrad placed his hands on the table. "She would tell us we're crazy and roll her eyes," he chimed in.

"But she would still be *all in*," Riley added.

"I wish I had known her better," Goldwein said quietly.

"We can honor her by finishing the job." Sullivan refocused them.

"Agreed," Conrad added.

"How did your prison visit go?" O'Keefe asked.

"We started a dialogue with Michael Wallace."

Conrad was skeptical. "He won't give us anything."

"Perhaps, but it's worth a shot," Sullivan answered.

"I know this will sound crazy, but what if Alexa Wallace got a job at the prison?" O'Keefe asked.

Conrad rolled his eyes playfully.

"Actually, just on the outside chance, I did check their employee roster while I was there. They only have five females working in the entire facility. None of them match our fugitive." Sullivan slammed the cell door on the topic.

"Where do we stand with Detective Dominguez?" Sullivan then asked.

"He has news." Conrad saw their ears perk up.

"What is it?" O'Keefe said eagerly.

"It turns out that he found a witness: the barkeep at the *Quencher* Tavern."

Conrad had their full attention.

"It turns out that the coyote was seen talking to a pair of junkies who live across the street from Fuller." He looked at each member of the team.

"And?" Sullivan finally asked.

"He is going to run it down. He can't find them."

"He will. Dominguez is dogged," Sullivan said flatly.

"Yes, he is."

"Keep us posted. I have a feeling it may be good old-fashioned detective work that might break this case in the end," Sullivan said.

"What is our next move?" Goldwein jumped in.

"You and I are going to repay a visit to the NSA."

"I told you *exactly* what Mr. Berlin said," Goldwein replied adamantly. "That avenue is closed."

"Not at all." Sullivan smiled. "That door is wide open."

"What are you going to do?" Riley asked.

"I'm going to make him an offer he can't refuse."

Not knowing Sullivan as well as the others, Goldwein was the only one who was confused rather than amused.

Having been briefed by Sullivan privately before the meeting, O'Keefe's eyes twinkled. Sullivan shot her a knowing look.

———

Alexa sat in the aisle seat of row twenty-two on her flight back to Washington, DC. Occasionally, she bent down to feel her bitten ankle, which she had treated again before the flight. The antibacterial ointment that she had applied was making her itch. She tried her best to ignore the discomfort.

Her mind drifted back to the Fortress. She recalled an incident when she was only nine years old. The family was on one of its drills, running through the woods. She had fallen, and Michael stopped to help her.

"What happened, Alexa?" he said, kneeling over her.

"I've banged my knee," she said, wincing.

"Never let pain stop you," he said, putting a comforting hand on her little head. The others ran on ahead without them.

"It hurts," she said.

"Think of your family when you are in pain," he said. "Think of how we all need you."

"But I'm just one. And I'm the littlest."

Michael put his hand up and stretched his fingers out.

"You see there are five fingers on a hand. You are one of the five fingers. Can a hand work as well with only four?" he asked.

"No," she answered quietly. "I'm the pinkie then."

Michael smiled. "Then let's go," he urged her.

Alexa got up and followed her brother. They ran like the wind.

———

The wake for Wesley Hughes was the largest in the history of Florence, Colorado. With just a skeleton crew at the prison, over a hundred officers wore their formal Bureau of Prison uniforms in honor of their fallen comrade. All members of the Florence Police Department, led by Chief LaPierre, were in attendance and stood as honor guards.

Warden Underwood gave a warm embrace to the members of Hughes's family. They had many questions for him earlier in the day, which he could not answer.

"How could this be?" Hughes's father had pleaded with him.

Chief LaPierre had told the family the results of the toxicology report. They were adamant that their son had no history of drug use. The warden could only say that the investigation was not over, and he would do his best to make sure the police kept digging. After the wake Warden Underwood met with Chief LaPierre and Captain Frye in the funeral home's parking lot.

"I'm telling you this is a homicide," Underwood started. "We drug test our employees, and Hughes was clean."

"I'm not disagreeing," the Chief added.

"The coroner said it was unusual that the overdose was entirely from fentanyl," Frye stated.

"How so?" Underwood was out of his element.

"Typically, drug dealers will add fentanyl to their heroin supply— to water it down. This didn't happen here."

The chief watched glumly as dozens of mourners streamed out of the funeral home.

"We will keep at it. The state police will also be conducting a review," LaPierre said, concluding their impromptu meeting.

Warden Underwood shook hands with LaPierre and Frye, thanking them both as he left. He knew that his duties now included informing BOP headquarters that he needed a replacement for Hughes. Whoever it was would have big shoes to fill.

After her long flight from Colorado finally landed, Alexa navigated her way toward the airport Metro station. She made a quick connection to the Silver Line. Once the Silver Line train's doors opened, she boarded and took a seat. It was Sunday afternoon, and there were plenty of empty places to sit. She chose a seat facing the direction of travel. She could not stand the seats that face backward. Those seats made her think of the past rather than the future. And while it was natural to reminisce, she thought that perhaps she was doing too much of it lately.

As she considered the events of the weekend, she thought of David Sutter. He had always been so thoughtful. Part of her was happy that she had spared him. Perhaps, she thought, he might still be useful. At the very least—she smiled to herself—he was a good cook.

Two seats ahead of her, a young couple held hands and whispered into each other's ears. Alexa watched the playful couple wistfully.

She wondered—what might she be doing if she had lived a normal life? In that other universe, she might not have a care in the world.

Alexa looked out the window as the train barreled forward, now above ground. Her reverie was eventually pierced by the sound of the conductor.

"Reston Station. Last stop!"

NINETEEN

NSA Revisited

The US Airways Shuttle, flight 2110 from Boston to Washington, was experiencing some serious turbulence. Goldwein sat next to Sullivan, hoping that the bumpy ride did not portend trouble on their mission. Her knuckles clung to both armrests like an eagle holding its prey in its talons. It bothered her that Sullivan seemed not to have a care in the world. He leaned his seat back, reading that day's edition of the *Boston Globe*.

"Are you going to tell me what you plan on telling Mr. Berlin?"

"It's best that you not know." Sullivan glanced over.

"I'd rather know."

"It's to protect you, believe me. By the way, what did you tell your supervisor?" Sullivan changed the subject without pretense.

"I had to take the only week of leave I have accumulated."

"Sorry," Sullivan offered.

"I was planning a cruise—now that is off, I guess."

"If our plan works, you will have to take more than a week, I'm guessing," Sullivan said seriously.

"That's all I have," she said, concerned.

"We will think of something." Sullivan seemed sure of himself.

"If you say so."

Goldwein tightened her grip on the armrests as the plane jerked up and down. Sullivan closed the newspaper and proceeded to take a nap.

⸺

The cavernous NSA visitors' center was not particularly welcoming, Sullivan thought to himself. He observed that it was built to give people the impression that they were most *unwelcome.* Sullivan and Goldwein sat patiently as Berlin was now more than thirty minutes late to their appointment. Sullivan looked at his watch, irritated.

"He is doing this on purpose."

"To make us feel he is in charge, right?" Goldwein asked.

"Yes."

"Well, it's working," Goldwein said shaking her head.

"It won't once I have a moment with him."

"You have to tell me what this is about," Goldwein insisted.

Sullivan grimaced and then leaned over conspiratorially. "After you read my question to him—"

"Yes, I remember." She cut him off.

"He was insulted personally. His concern was for *his* privacy, not the public's privacy."

Goldwein thought back to how Berlin had gotten so upset. How he had turned red. She remembered his words: *I have an expectation of privacy that the police will not pry into my home, my bedroom.*

"Oh my God, you are going to blackmail him!" Her hands went to her face.

"I call it persuasion."

"I can't be part of this." Goldwein stood up.

At that moment, Berlin bounded out of a door and into the visitors' room.

Sullivan turned to Goldwein quickly. "Please trust me. Wait here. We will discuss further."

She shook her head and sat down.

"My partner will wait here, Mr. Berlin."

"Very well," Berlin said as he escorted Sullivan toward his office.

Sullivan looked back once more and mouthed *thank you* as he walked away.

———

Fifteen minutes later, Sullivan walked out of the same door he had entered; only this time he was alone. He walked toward Goldwein, who was visibly stewing.

"Let's go," he said without stopping.

She got up and walked out to the parking lot with him.

"We aren't done with this conversation." Goldwein raised her voice.

"No, we're not," he answered.

"You can't just blackmail people." She pointed down at the ground aggressively.

"I didn't blackmail people. I blackmailed someone who is engaging in Internet shenanigans, to say the least."

"How can you be so sure?"

"The Russians have a saying,"

"Oh here we go again." Goldwein was flustered.

"Trust but verify," he said.

"What does that even mean?"

"That I had O'Keefe dig into Berlin's Internet use just to verify my suspicions."

"Oh my God! Now you have O'Keefe breaking the law, too." She shook her head.

"O'Keefe made a decision that she will do what it takes to avenge Fuller." Sullivan stared at her hard.

"We have to follow the law, Sully."

Sullivan paused at her words. He knew in his heart that she was right. Yet he would not be stopped.

"Look Suzanne." His tone softened.

"What?"

"I really need you on this mission. We are so close."

"But we are breaking the law."

"What if I make you a promise?" he asked.

"What?" She was intrigued.

"When this is over, I will turn myself in. I will take full responsibility. You can even hand me over yourself."

"You will let me arrest you?" Her eyes arched.

"Yes. You can take me in."

Goldwein pondered his proposal. As impassioned as she was in the pursuit of lawful justice, she wanted to make history as Sullivan had earlier promised her. He seemed so sure of their path.

"Deal," she said finally.

He reached over and shook her hand.

"So," she said, "how did it go in there?"

"You start tomorrow. You will have full access."

"Oh my God, it worked!"

"Of course!" He slapped her on the shoulder.

"I'm going to be like a kid in a candy store in there." She laughed.

"Do you hear that sound, Goldwein?" he asked, a hand cupping his ear.

"What sound?"

"Champagne, Goldwein. I hear champagne uncorking."

TWENTY

Changes

Two days after Hughes's funeral, Captain Sanders summoned Alexa into his office. She had been anticipating the call and was glad when it finally came.

She walked into his office, and again Sanders was on the phone. It was becoming comical. She took a seat without being instructed as this was becoming routine.

"Yes, Vince," Sanders bellowed, "I know, but I'm convinced the Capitals will be in the playoffs, no doubt."

Alexa did not follow sports teams, but she knew enough that she could tell he was talking about professional hockey. After sitting patiently for almost ten minutes, Sanders finally hung up the phone.

"Amanda," he started, "I have good news and bad news."

Her heart sank. Could they have given Hughes's position to someone else?

"What is the bad news?" she asked.

"There was a tragic death in Florence. One of our officers died last week."

"Oh, my goodness, that is horrible." Alexa feigned concern. "How did he die?" she inquired.

"It appears to be a drug overdose, but you didn't hear that from me," he said sternly.

"Understood, Captain."

"The one positive thing, of course, is that this clears the way for your hardship transfer." He shuffled some papers on his desk as he talked.

"When do I begin?"

"In less than two weeks. You report for duty on Monday, May first," he said.

"I can do that, sir, and thank you."

"This will be a good change for you, Amanda. But I want you to know that you will be missed."

"That is nice to know." Alexa smiled.

"By tradition, we will take you out to lunch on your last day, if that works for you."

"Yes, I'm honored." She beamed.

As she walked out of his office and down the hallway, she considered what a wonderful omen it was to be transferred on May 1, known as *May Day*. It was a day of communist celebration worldwide. It was a day when the oppressed workers stood up and shouted against oppressive governments of the world. She was sure this was a sign of success to come. She had an extra bounce in her step as she walked to her cubicle.

———

Michael Wallace stared at his newly prized possession, his watch, and felt it for the hundredth time. After accepting the deal with Sullivan, he had cursed himself a dozen times. During his service in the Iraq War, Wallace had participated in many interrogations. He was familiar with the dueling theories concerning successful interrogations.

One camp argued that coercive techniques were best suited to quickly gather useful information from hardened detainees. This could include waterboarding and other stressful methods. The other camp disagreed, siding with the FBI interrogation manual, which stressed rapport-based techniques. This side felt that coercive methods only made subjects lie to stop the discomfort.

In Michael's experience both sides were correct, inasmuch as no single approach could fit all situations. Some hardened subjects could only be broken through stressful methods. However, he agreed with the FBI that most subjects are susceptible to a more subtle approach. This could include treating the subject with respect, as Sullivan had done with him. It could also involve deception, as he suspected was the case concerning his sister.

Michael kicked himself because it had worked on him. After being subjected to isolation for so long, he welcomed Sullivan's gesture. Sullivan had played him like a violin. Yet he was a lonely violin.

He had consoled himself with the knowledge that the watch brought him some useful changes. He could now time the meals delivered by the guards to exactly 6.5-hour intervals. He now knew the guards conducted cell checks every thirty minutes. It gave him a measure of control. He knew exactly how long he slept and when his meals would be arriving. He was not sure if the watch was set for Mountain Time, but it was close. He could tell from the sun above his cell that it was within one hour of accuracy.

Perhaps the watch would give him an edge when the time was right. He glanced at it once more as he prepared to take a nap. He looked up at the darkening sky. He could faintly see a crescent moon behind a cloud. He wondered if his sister was any closer to finding him. This was his last thought as he dozed off.

TWENTY ONE

Breakthrough

Supervisory Special Agent Bill Walker was beyond frustrated. He had no new leads in the death of Agent Fuller. Her homicide was inextricably linked to the Coyote investigation given that Alexa Wallace was their lead murder suspect. Essentially, both investigations were one and the same. The director had asked him for daily updates, and he had precious little to show. He knew that he needed to show results soon, or the director would remove him as quickly as he had taken Sullivan off the case. In that vein he had ordered a squad of agents from headquarters to recanvass Fuller's neighbors.

Detective Dominguez watched from his unmarked cruiser as FBI agents knocked on doors on Fuller's street. Few doors opened for the agents. Those that did produced no new leads. Dominguez had Turner's apartment in his sights as two FBI agents talked to Jody Turner on her doorstep. After a minute or so, he could see her shake her head, and the agents walked away. Once they were out of sight, Dominguez headed for her door, a bag of groceries in his hands.

"Mrs. Turner," Dominguez said as she answered her door again.

"Yes, Detective." She looked down the street, checking to see if the agents were gone.

"I brought some groceries," he said, handing her the bag.

"Oh, my." She blushed. "You didn't need to do that!"

"I know times are tough, ma'am," he said.

"Thank you so much. I don't know what to say," she replied gratefully.

"Don't worry about it." He turned to leave.

"Thanks again." She waved at him as he walked away.

Dominguez never asked about her son, Sonny, or his girlfriend, Tammy. He knew he didn't have to.

—

A week had elapsed and Sullivan had not heard from Goldwein. He had told her to economize her contacts with the team. She didn't need to report every advance she made. It would only attract attention from NSA employees, who would be naturally suspicious of her. He only needed her to call when she had actionable intelligence. It was best that she keep as low a profile as possible, he had counseled her.

Prior to leaving her in Maryland, Sullivan had given Goldwein a disposable cell phone. Likewise, he had a burner phone of his own for exclusive contact with her. Just as he had spied on Berlin, Sullivan wanted to make sure Berlin could not return the favor. He knew Berlin had been wounded. And he knew that a wounded animal could strike back. He was concerned that Berlin might start spying on the team's telephones.

Sullivan sat across from O'Keefe and Conrad when his cell phone lit up. He smiled as he saw that it was Goldwein.

"I think I have something," she said, standing in the NSA parking lot.

"Where is she?" he asked, leaning forward anxiously.

"Reston, Virginia, Sullivan."

"Excellent, Goldwein,"

"She's using the computers at the Reston Public Library." Goldwein glanced about nervously.

"That makes perfect sense," he muttered.

"She's certain we can't track her from public sites."

"So she's in for a surprise," he said, getting Conrad's attention.

"It gets better, Sully."

"How so?" He arched his eyes.

"She seems to conduct her searches on Saturdays."

"That's tomorrow." He looked at his watch, mentally checking to see when he could be in Washington.

"I will pick you up at the airport," Goldwein offered, anticipating Sullivan's next move.

"We'll be on the next flight." He turned off the phone and leapt out of his chair.

Conrad grabbed his jacket, kissed O'Keefe, and loyally followed his partner out the door.

———

Alexa's last day at the office was a festive affair. Not only was it a Friday, but it had also given her colleagues something to celebrate. In a large bureaucracy, every employee milestone is acknowledged. It is a cost-effective way of boosting office morale. Captain Sanders had organized a lunch at *Fernando's Cantina,* two blocks from their office.

Alexa sat next to Betty Spicer and across from her mentor, Captain Sanders. Eight other members of the Intelligence Unit were also seated around the long rectangular table. At the center Spicer had placed a chocolate cake that she had baked the night before.

After eating their meals, Sanders stood up, automatically silencing the small talk around the table.

"I want to thank Amanda for her work at the unit," he started.

"I second that," Spicer interrupted.

"She will be missed. But our loss will be Florence's gain."

"Speech!" her colleagues shouted.

Alexa reluctantly got up from her seat.

"I just want to thank all of you. The way you welcomed me was just so sweet." She said what she knew they wanted to hear.

As Spicer cut the cake, Alexa thought about all the work ahead of her. She was leaving for Colorado the next day, and she wasn't done packing. She also wanted to stop at the library before leaving. She wanted to print out a set of *Mapquest* directions for her long trip.

Alexa was eager to start her journey.

TWENTY TWO

Showdown

The sun seemed to have extra wattage on that late-April, Saturday morning. Conrad pushed his sunglasses tighter to his nose to limit the glare. Agents Rogers and Wheeler had volunteered to join their fugitive hunt, and they leaned against the rental car piloted by Goldwein. Riley had his hands in his pocket as he looked about. He and the others were wearing clothing to conceal their weapons as surprise was their most potent weapon for this operation.

The team had conducted a drive-by surveillance of the library in their two rental cars to familiarize themselves with the area. They were now two blocks from the Reston Public Library.

Sullivan had placed a large piece of paper on the hood of his rental car. The team stood around him.

"According to Goldwein," Sullivan started, "Wallace researched information about the team, *especially Fuller*, from the computers in the library."

"That's right." Goldwein nodded.

"We have to assume she has pictures of me and Conrad."

"Great," Conrad muttered.

"But the rest of you should be unknown to her."

They shook their heads.

"The only person in the library will be Suzanne." He pointed at Goldwein.

"I will be your eyes and ears inside," she offered.

"Rogers and Wheeler, thanks for playing today." Sullivan looked at them. "Let's put you in car number one, at this corner." He marked the map with his pen for them. "Riley, let's have you reading a book at this bench, right outside the entrance." He again marked his sketch.

"What about me?" Conrad asked.

"You and I will be in vehicle two, at this corner," he said.

"What about communications?" Wheeler asked.

Sullivan looked at Riley, the tech agent on the team. Riley reached into a small bag and handed them each a *Bluetooth* earpiece.

"We will have a four-way conference call going for the entire surveillance," Riley said to the team.

"Real-time communication," Sullivan declared.

"I hope you all brought chargers," Conrad added.

They all nodded.

"So what's the plan?" Goldwein asked.

"Simple," Sullivan started. "Once you have her at a computer terminal, we will all converge at once and jump her. We have overwhelming numbers."

"And if she doesn't come to a terminal?" Goldwein looked around to all the team members.

"Once she's inside, if she wanders around, you will keep us posted. Then we will wait for her outside."

"And jump her as she comes out," Riley chimed in.

"Sounds good," Conrad exclaimed.

They all looked at Sullivan.

"The library opens in an hour, so let's check our weapons, use the restrooms, and get ready."

Sullivan looked at his watch. He could feel victory approaching.

———

Mr. Klingman was not pleased when Alexa told him that she was moving out. A vacancy meant once more advertising for the unit, hoping to find a reliable tenant. He thought that Alexa was a model tenant. No parties. No noises. And she paid her rent in a timely manner.

After inspecting her unit, he found that she was leaving it in immaculate condition. He was very strict about these matters, but he could see she had taken time to do a good job. He found this impressive and unusual in a young person.

"I'm sorry you are leaving," he remarked as he handed her $1,500 in cash—her security deposit.

"Thank you," she said softly, walking out the door to the street.

He looked at her for the last time as she walked away. She wore sneakers with blue jeans and a white top. Her shoulder-length hair was loose and straight. It was warm enough that she did not need a jacket. In her back pocket, Alexa had placed a folded white ball cap.

Alexa walked to her blue Ford F-150 pickup truck and checked the tarp once more. She had tied down her belongings on the bed of the truck, and she wanted to make sure everything was secure. Rather than fight for a parking spot at the library, she decided to walk there. Her leg had healed remarkably well with the treatments she had administered.

The sun was out, and it was a beautiful day. She knew she would be in the truck for several hours once her journey commenced. This would prove to be her only exercise of the day, or so she believed.

———

Conrad and Sullivan sat in their vehicle in silence for several minutes. Neither of them liked to chitchat needlessly, especially when they were focused on an operation. Further, they were on a conference call with the rest of the team, and they didn't need any needless distractions. Eventually, however, Conrad broke the silence.

"What else did Goldwein learn at the NSA?"

"She used the same computers to research Michael Wallace and the ADX Supermax where he is being kept." Sullivan glared at the library entrance.

Conrad could feel Sullivan's intensity. Goldwein's ears perked up as she listened.

"That makes sense; she's looking for information on her brother."

"So it would seem,"

"Anything else?" Conrad inquired.

"It's hard to tell because so many people use those computers. She can't attribute any other searches to the coyote definitively."

"Except the obvious ones—I get it," Conrad said.

"From the fact that she comes here on Saturdays, we can assume she has a traditional nine-to-five weekday job."

The team listened to the conversation with interest.

A silence fell over the car as people started stirring about. They watched as a group of youngsters were escorted by an elderly couple into the library. That group was followed by three middle-aged men entering separately. A minute later, a gray sedan pulled into the parking lot. Conrad pointed at the car with his chin.

"Let's see," Sullivan said, waiting.

After an interminable minute, a female in her thirties got out of the car, a stack of books under her arm.

"Crap," Sullivan said.

Conrad frowned.

Just as Conrad was about to say something, Sullivan spotted her. It was not her age or size that gave her away. It was her confident stride, as if she were gliding, that caught his attention.

He nudged Conrad with his elbow. She was a block away and walking perpendicular to their position. As she crossed the street, they noticed her looking in their direction. However, they knew the solar glare on the windshield prevented her from seeing them inside the car.

"Listen up, everyone. I think she's here," Sullivan called out.

———

Alexa approached the library with her usual caution. Despite her conviction that she could not be traced to that location, she practiced the same countersurveillance methods that were second nature to her. She scanned the area, looking for anything that was out of place. As she approached the library, she noticed a car on the corner. Although she could not see inside, she could hear that the engine was running. Interesting, she thought. This was her first observation.

As she climbed the four steps to the library door, she noticed a middle-aged male sitting at a picnic table just outside the entrance. He was reading a paperback book and wearing a *Bluetooth* earpiece. Riley was doing his best to look uninterested. Still, she noticed that he was wearing a long jacket on a warm spring day. This was her second observation.

Alexa entered the library and walked toward the Internet-access area on the left, past the main desk. Her radar was now on full alert, so she quickened her pace. She immediately noticed a young female was the only patron using an Internet station. More to the point, she was *appearing* to use the computer when she was actually looking right at her. And she was wearing a *Bluetooth* earpiece. As Alexa walked toward her, she watched the woman's mouth carefully.

"She's coming toward me," Suzanne whispered quietly.

Alexa read her lips easily. She needed no further observations.

As Alexa walked toward Suzanne, she grabbed a large hard-cover book from one of the stacks. She did so in one fluid movement without pausing. Suzanne didn't even notice. Alexa lunged at Suzanne, smashing the book into her face, knocking her back unconscious.

The team could hear something had happened.

"Are you all right, Suzanne?" Sullivan asked.

Alexa quickly leaned over and grabbed the earpiece, putting it on. She reached into Suzanne's pocket and took her phone, putting it in her back pocket. The attack was swift and vicious. The sound of the book crashing into Suzanne's face was not particularly loud. The only patron within twenty feet of them didn't even notice.

Alexa found Suzanne's holster and tried prying her pistol from her, but could not. It was a hardened holster in which the gun slides and locks into place. She quickly realized getting the gun would take too much time and gave up.

Alexa walked quickly toward the restrooms on the far end of the library. As she did, she could hear Sullivan in her ear.

"Suzanne, report please!"

"I'm OK," Alexa said. "It wasn't her."

The group's anxiousness subsided for a moment. As their tension eased for a second, Alexa entered the women's restroom.

Sullivan and Conrad suddenly looked at each other. They had the same simultaneous thought flash through their heads.

"Riley!" Sullivan yelled. "Suzanne's in trouble! Get in there!"

Riley dashed into the library. Conrad and Sullivan jumped out of their cars and sprinted toward the entrance. Alexa could hear that they were now in full pursuit. She unlocked the restroom window and opened it enough to get outside.

"Wheeler, Rogers, wait outside in case she leaves the building!"

Riley got to Suzanne, who was now starting to stir from unconsciousness.

"Suzanne is down!" he yelled, kneeling over her.

"Take care of her, Riley! Get her to a hospital!" Sullivan said as he entered the building.

Sullivan and Conrad were in the library, guns out, searching through the stacks for their fugitive. Several patrons started screaming and ran for the exit. As Conrad and Sullivan split up to widen their search, Alexa was already outside.

"I see her!" Wheeler said.

Rogers, in the passenger seat, drew his weapon. Alexa was about to cross the street in front of them. Alexa had the advantage of hearing her pursuers. She knew their intentions.

"I'm running her over," Wheeler yelled.

He gunned the engine and barreled toward her in the middle of the street. The car was within three feet of her when Alexa somersaulted in the air, landing cleanly on the trunk as the car screeched to a stop.

"What the fuck!" Rogers screamed, not believing his eyes.

Alexa jumped down and started running.

Sullivan and Conrad were now running past Rogers and Wheeler's vehicle, which had to try and awkwardly turn around. As they ran after her, they could see she was much faster than them. She was now more than a quarter of a mile away. Alexa ran like a gazelle.

Alexa, as a Reston resident, also had the advantage of knowing the area. She ran toward a large strip mall. She knew that on a beautiful Saturday morning, *Winchester's*, a large local clothing store, would be chock-full of people. She had shopped there herself on many occasions and knew it well.

As she approached the store, Alexa looked back and saw Sullivan and Conrad in the distance as a car pulled up to them. She could hear nothing from the earpiece. She surmised that they now had realized she was monitoring them. Sullivan and Conrad jumped into the backseat of the vehicle, which was now headed toward her at full speed.

As Alexa walked into the store, she pulled out her baseball cap and put it on her head. She made sure that her pursuers saw her do it. With no weapon and outnumbered, she knew she would have to use all of her skills, training, and ingenuity.

———

Riley was at Goldwein's side when the emergency medical technicians from the Reston Hospital arrived to help. The hospital was on the same street as the library, four blocks away, so their arrival was nearly instantaneous. They had to navigate around two dozen confused patrons and library staff to enter the building.

Suzanne was groggy but responsive when they questioned her. They quickly evaluated her as suffering from a concussion. As the EMTs put her on a stretcher, the Reston Police arrived.

"I'm Officer Streeter," he said to Riley. "What happened here?"

"I'm Special Agent Tom Riley, FBI." He displayed his credentials.

"Is she with you?" he asked as his partner stood next to him.

"She's also an FBI agent," he said. He was not sure how much to tell the officers.

"So what happened?" the officer asked, flustered.

"We were trying to apprehend a fugitive, and she got away."

"A fugitive? In the library?" Officer Streeter was perplexed.

"It's complicated."

"I'm calling my supervisor," Streeter said, reaching for his radio.

"That's not really necessary," Riley pleaded.

"Yeah, it is," the officer answered sternly.

———

When conducting surveillance, it is human nature to take mental short-cuts. Events occur quickly in a mobile surveillance, and it is impossible to lock in on specific features—especially when the person being followed is in a public area. So it is natural to focus in on something distinctive, like a red-headed person or the color of a piece of clothing, such as the color of a person's hat. This tendency has been noted in countersurveillance training by terrorists and spies for decades. It is a human weakness to be exploited by the hunted.

Alexa entered the store and quickly headed toward the women's section.

Outside, Wheeler pulled their car directly in front of the store's entrance.

"She's wearing a white hat," he said as he put the car in park.

"Conrad, wait here with Rogers," Sullivan said.

Conrad understood his friend's intentions.

"I need you to wait for Riley and coordinate with the local police. I'm sure they will be here soon." Sullivan put his hand on Conrad's shoulder.

"We'll watch the door, Sully."

"Wheeler, let's go."

Sullivan and Wheeler entered the store through the automatic doors. Their first thought was that there must be at least a hundred people milling about. The ambient noise was quite loud. It was a big store. Sullivan went left, and Wheeler right.

Alexa quickly found the hat section and swapped her white hat for a red one. She then walked to a rack of sports clothing, quickly grabbing a burgundy-and-gold Redskins football jersey. She knelt down behind the rack and put it on over her blouse. The Jersey still had a security tag attached to it. She did not try and remove it. She knew it would not matter.

Alexa then moved to the men's section and found a rack of suits. She removed one suit from the rack, and threw it on the floor. The hanger was made of wood, and it had a metal hook. She placed the hanger on the floor, and using her foot, she bent the hook back so it was not as curved. She grabbed her new weapon and knelt to the floor, looking for the agents from below.

After a few moments, she noticed a pair of feet approaching tentatively. As the man got closer, Alexa stood up and put her back to the agent. She could hear him behind her as she pretended to browse through the rack of clothing. The agent saw her attire and decided to walk past her.

Once he passed her, she turned to him. She could not tell which agent it was with his back to her, but it didn't matter. He was the enemy. She could see him scanning the area in front of him, his gun out at waist level pointing to the floor.

"Excuse me," Alexa called out to him.

As he swung around to face her, Alexa, coiled like a springboard, swung her weapon at his face. The hook connected with the agent's eye, and blood splattered over his face as he fell back in agony. He screamed out as he lay on his back, immobilized. His service weapon lay at his side on the floor. Shock had started to set in.

—

Captain Roy Vinson of the Reston Police Department arrived at the hospital as Goldwein was being evaluated by an emergency-room doctor. Officer Streeter had sounded quite agitated when he called for his assistance, and he was visibly relieved at his captain's quick response. Prior to his career in law enforcement, Vinson had been a star running back on his college football team. He had learned the importance of speed in critical situations. The report he received was sketchy, but it involved FBI agents and drama at the library. He could tell it was not going to be an ordinary day.

In the time it took the captain to reach the hospital, Riley had already made the decision to tell the local police the truth. Not only was it the right thing to do, but they might also be able to help find their fugitive. As far as Riley knew, the hunt was still on.

Vinson shook his head as Riley quickly filled him in on the team's plan and what went wrong. Officer Streeter stood at Vinson's side as they heard the full story.

"If you had only told us beforehand, this would not have happened," Vinson scolded Riley.

"It's a little late for that, Captain. I'm sorry."

"So where is the rest of your team?"

"They took off after her. I don't know."

Vinson reached for his phone to inform the chief, when his radio crackled.

"Captain, we have reports of shots fired!"

He recognized the voice as his department's police dispatcher, Kelly Welch. He could hear the tension in her voice. Reston did not have any shootings.

"Where?" Vinson radioed back.

"*Winchester's*, Captain."

"I guess we found your team," Vinson said flatly as he turned to leave.

Riley had never felt as helpless as he did that moment. He felt his chest tighten.

—

Alexa quickly grabbed the fallen agent's pistol and started shooting in the air. The pop-pop-pop of gunfire pierced the noisy store. She then ran through the store past the largest cluster of customers.

"Man with a gun!" she yelled.

Hearing the gunshots, not everyone knew exactly what they were hearing. Most patrons were puzzled at first. Alexa tried again.

"He's shooting us!" she yelled. "Everybody out!"

Suddenly, the gunshots combined with Alexa's screams got their attention. Sensing danger, the customers started to panic. Scores of patrons rushed the doors, Alexa among them.

Sullivan, hearing the gunfire, ran to the side of the store that Wheeler was covering. After checking several clothing racks, he found Wheeler on the ground, one hand over his wounded eye. Next to him was a bloody coat hanger. He kneeled down to Wheeler, who was whispering something unintelligible. Sullivan feared Wheeler was going into shock.

He grabbed Wheeler's free hand and held on tight. His skin was turning pale and clammy.

"It looks like you've lost an eye, Wheeler, but you will survive."

Sullivan knew that in a situation where someone has suffered a serious wound, the last thing a victim should be told is that "everything will be all right." People who are dying are told this routinely. So instead of calming a person, a wounded person hearing this assumes they are doomed and gives up hope. It is better to be direct about the seriousness of the injury and the prospect for recovery.

Wheeler moaned quietly. "You think I will make it, Sully?" he whispered.

"Absolutely," Sullivan reassured him.

"But my eye—"

"The eye doesn't look good, Wheeler,"

As he spoke, he knew that his fugitive was on her way out of the store. Yet he could not leave Wheeler's side. His hope rested on Conrad catching her outside.

———

Conrad and Rogers had guarded the store's entrance, refusing entry to any new patrons once Sullivan and Wheeler went inside. A few customers had exited in small groups at first, but Conrad scrutinized each one before they were allowed to leave. Now, however, a crush of patrons was fleeing the store, overwhelming them. As the group ran out, some of the customers were screaming. Group panic had taken hold.

Alexa placed her new pistol in her waistband, covering it with her football jersey. The security tag on the jersey sounded an alarm as she was leaving, but in the commotion and panic, it was not an issue. Everyone was focused on leaving immediately.

Squeezing in between two larger customers, Alexa came out of the store with the multitudes. She could see Conrad and Rogers looking about frantically. She noticed that they were looking at everyone's heads. They were looking for a white hat.

Alexa, in her red hat, walked through the crowd and to the perimeter of the parking lot. As she walked away, she could hear the sounds of police sirens approaching.

———

Upon being informed that shots were reportedly fired at *Winchester's*, Captain Vinson had called for ambulances to follow his cruiser to the store. All five of his department's cruisers that were on duty for that shift were also dispatched. As they pulled up to *Winchester's*, Sullivan, Conrad, and Rogers were carrying Wheeler out of the store. The EMTs quickly pulled out a stretcher, and they placed Wheeler on it gently. Rogers stayed with him as they put him in the ambulance.

"I'm Captain Vinson. Agent Riley briefed me."

"I'm Agent Sullivan"—he waved to Jimmy—"and this is Agent Conrad."

"How bad is your man?" Vinson asked.

"He lost an eye," Sullivan said in disgust.

"And the fugitive?"

"She got away," Conrad jumped in.

Vinson had recognized Sullivan from the Coyote press conference. He had heard that Sullivan could be a wild card.

"I had heard you were taken off the case." Vinson looked at Sullivan suspiciously.

"Technically, I suppose."

"I see." Vinson arched his eyebrows.

"Captain, can you pull the video for the store?" Conrad asked.

"I suppose."

"That would be great," Conrad added.

"So this coyote has been living in Reston the whole time?" Vinson asked.

"I would have to say yes." Sullivan looked down, his fists clenched.

He bit his lip as he watched the ambulance with Wheeler pull away. He then looked at Captain Vinson.

"This isn't over, Captain."

Vinson looked at Sullivan's face and saw the conviction in his eyes. He had the look of a quarterback who had just been intercepted on a big play but knew he would still win the game.

———

A mile away, back in her quiet neighborhood, Alexa slid into her pickup truck, which was gassed up and ready to go. She threw the baseball cap on the floor of the cab. She left the jersey on as her pursuers had last seen her wearing a white blouse. She would dispose of the jersey later.

Shifting into drive, she pulled out, and using side roads, she purposely avoided any toll roads, which might have cameras. Alexa knew that the FBI would start checking those cameras around the time frame of the incident.

The directional compass on her dashboard signaled a clear W. She was headed west.

TWENTY THREE

Traveler

The town of Casey, Iowa, is nothing more than a small dot on a map. With fewer than five hundred residents, it is hardly worthy of a visit from the census bureau. It is, however, strategically located in the central part of the state, on Interstate 80, which dissects Iowa in half. Travelers heading west to the Rockies or east to Chicago and further to the Atlantic are familiar with the signs for Casey for one simple reason: lodging.

The highway cutting past the sleepy town is dotted with motels of various sizes and reputations. Some of the cheaper lodging establishments were frequented by drifters and truckers, which quickly attracted a number of regular working girls.

The *Route 80 Bar and Grill* was a short walk from some of the motels, and a short car ride from all of them. The neon bar sign blinked periodically in the darkness. Because of the transient nature of the area, it was quite common to see license plates from all over the United States in town. For this reason Alexa's pickup truck from Virginia merited zero attention from those who passed by. From her elevated perch in her pickup truck's driver's seat, she had the bar under a discreet observation.

To pass the time, she would occasionally turn her attention to the flat Iowa countryside visible on the other side of the highway. The scenery was intermittently illuminated by a passing lightning storm several miles away. Alexa rolled her window down to enjoy the fresh air. Despite the tempest in the distance, she could smell no rain in the air, and the wind was still. This told her it was not a threatening storm.

On her radio Alexa had tuned the dial to a mellow country-music station. The disc jockey had just announced that it was ten o'clock.

She turned her attention to the bar again, waiting.

—

The lights on the seven[th] floor of the FBI's Hoover Building were shining brightly and visible to any pedestrian outside that might stop and take notice. This was unusual for that time of night. Even the most dedicated employees were usually gone by nine. However, the Reston incident had roiled the Bureau's management. Director Anthony Franklin sat behind his desk, his four top deputies seated in front of him. He listened as his underlings engaged in an animated conversation.

"We need to keep a lid on this entire episode," one said.

"I know some reporters at the *Washington Post.* I can ask for a favor," another agreed.

"We need to immediately increase the size of the team here at headquarters," still another added.

The director finally spoke. "You are losing sight of something very important."

The comment hung in the air for a moment. One of them finally responded.

"What is that, sir?"

"They almost caught her, didn't they?"

They all nodded.

"That's more progress than the official team has made from what I can see."

"Yes, sir, but their methods were not exactly legal from what I'm hearing," one replied.

"I need to tell the president that we can catch this fugitive. I'm having to make excuses every time I give him an intelligence briefing." Franklin wiped his brow.

"Are you suggesting we transfer the case back to Sullivan?" one incredulous deputy asked.

"No, not at all. Suspend Sullivan and his whole team."

They stared at him, confused by the seemingly contradictory message.

"Sir?" one finally asked, puzzled.

"They aren't going to be stopped. By suspending them, they can take the gloves off."

"And if it goes sideways, we can deny involvement," one proposed.

The director leaned back in his large chair. He smiled, realizing his deputy only saw the glass as half empty. He pointed at the deputy like a teacher.

"And if they succeed, we can embrace them again."

———

Alexa perked up in her seat as two male patrons walked out of the *Route 80 Bar and Grill.* She estimated them to be approximately thirty years old. Both seemed physically fit. Perfect, she thought.

She watched as they talked outside of a parked car. One of them pointed down the road, possibly to where he was staying. After a couple of minutes, they fist bumped one another. One of them got in a Toyota Camry with Illinois license plates and started the engine. He pulled onto the highway and headed east, toward Chicago she surmised.

The other man walked west toward a series of motels. Alexa got out of her truck and started following him on foot. She gradually got closer to him until he finally heard her approaching.

"Hello," he said, his eyes widening.

"Hi there, cowboy," she answered.

The drinks in his system made him bolder than he would ordinarily act. He was not sure if she was a prostitute or just a friendly girl. He decided it didn't matter. He wanted company.

"Are you from around here?"

"No, just passing through," she answered.

"Do you want a drink? I have some beer in my room."

"Sure."

"Follow me."

He quickened the pace as they walked to the nearby two-story *Comfort Inn*. The rooms faced the parking lot. He had a room on the first floor. Alexa looked around before following him into the room. She saw nobody watching them.

As soon as he closed the door, she brutally punched him in the throat, crushing his Adam's apple. He started gasping for air in a panic. She grabbed his arm and helped him to the floor.

"You'll be OK," she said as he stared up at her in pain.

She quickly turned him on his side and handcuffed him.

"You will be fine," she reassured him as he finally started breathing again.

Again, grabbing him by the arm, she helped him off the floor and onto a chair. She then pulled a carefully measured dose of fentanyl out of her pocket and placed it on the table. She then retrieved her pistol from her waistband and also laid it in front of them. Her message was unmistakable.

"What's your name?" she asked.

"Tim."

"OK, Tim, I need you to take something."

"Sure, whatever," he said, shaking.

"But first, how many drinks did you have?"

"I had three beers," he answered, confused.

"All right then, Tim. We will wait a couple of hours. I need you sober."

Alexa then calmly reached over and grabbed the TV remote control.

———

The next morning, the maid at the *Comfort Inn* found Tim dead in his bed. His restraints had been removed. The Iowa State Patrol was called, and a homicide investigation was initiated, despite the fact that it appeared to be an overdose death. It was police protocol.

State police detectives had no way to connect such a random death to the search for the elusive coyote fugitive.

TWENTY FOUR

Dinner and Dreams

Michael Wallace glanced at his watch. He knew his meal would be arriving in exactly ten minutes. Like one of Pavlov's dogs, he had started to salivate. Not because the food was tasteful. Indeed, on most days, the meals tasted like cardboard. Instead, his delight was in the distraction it provided from the grinding monotony. It was something to entertain his mind.

He had already built two homes from top to bottom in his mental calisthenics. He realized that perhaps he was building them too quickly. In the future he decided he would pay more attention to detail. Perhaps, he would furnish the homes as well. That thought consoled him for a few minutes while he waited to be fed like a dog in a kennel.

After the food arrived, his face turned dour. He had been hoping for at least some fruit. On occasion he was given an orange or an apple. Those meals gave him something to celebrate. This time he was served a stale piece of bread and a ham-and-cheese sandwich. The cheese smelled as if it had been left to bake under a hot desert sun. Still, he ate it. What else was there to do? As he chewed on his meal, his thoughts again turned to his sister. Was she in a similar predicament as Agent Sullivan had suggested? Or was she in a better place?

As the days turned to weeks and the weeks to months, he started to wonder if she had forgotten him. He took one last swallow and prepared to take a nap.

———

Alexa leaned forward to pour herself another glass of merlot. She rarely drank alcohol, but she had started to enjoy David Sutter's selections of wine. After her adventure in Virginia on the day of her departure, she was enjoying the way it made her relax. She leaned back on the couch and slowly swirled the wine in her glass.

Sutter had prepared her a sumptuous meal of chicken cordon bleu with jasmine rice and asparagus. The chicken had been cooked to perfection. It seemed to melt in her mouth. The rice had a tinge of saffron, and the asparagus had been lightly dipped in butter.

From his living room, Alexa watched as he rinsed the last dish and walked over to the couch. He sat down next to her and poured himself another glass of wine.

"Do you like it?" he asked as the last of the wine settled into his glass.

"Very much."

"I'm glad."

"It doesn't seem fair though," Alexa said.

"What do you mean?"

"You spent all day helping me move into my new apartment, so I'm the one who should be cooking for you." She smiled at him.

"You had a long drive from back East," he said. "You've earned a little relaxation."

"You are sweet," she said, touching him gently on the face.

They talked for another hour. Sutter had made plans for Alexa to meet his parents, and she had agreed. Once she decided to spare his life, Alexa thought she would make the most of the situation. He was turning out to be an amazing asset.

When it was time to leave, Sutter walked Alexa to her truck. Before leaving, she gave him a long kiss good-night. It was the least she could do, she thought. She drove off with the vague realization that she was starting to have feelings for him.

——

Sullivan looked down at his meal, and his shoulders slumped. The lasagna leftovers he pulled from his refrigerator had not heated well. The pasta had gotten hard around the edges. He had microwaved it and now he was scraping it from the plastic container onto a thin paper plate. The red sauce had formed a puddle in the middle of the plate, causing it to sag. He barely got the plate onto his kitchen table in one piece. He stared at the meal with the weight of the world on his shoulders.

Sullivan now had to answer for one agent getting a concussion and another losing an eye. He had played his best hand and lost. He reflected on how he had underestimated his opponent. She was more formidable than he had ever considered. As he started to pick at his food, he thought that he didn't deserve a better meal yet. He would have to earn it.

After his meal Sullivan decided to go to bed early. The team had been summoned for a meeting by Special Agent in Charge (SAC) Whitworth. His supervisor, Jonathan Waters, had called him with the bad news. Although Waters was in his corner, this was beyond his ability to squash. He told Sullivan that the punishments had been decided at the highest level in the Bureau. He knew this meant the director himself was involved. Sullivan was prepared to take full responsibility. His team had suffered enough. No matter what happened, he knew the game was far from over.

His opponent was on the run, and he was a patient hunter. This was his last thought as he fell asleep.

——

Michael Wallace snored gently. He had grown accustomed to sleeping on his back. He had tried several different sleeping positions in his bunk, and that was the most comfortable for him. Lying on his side caused his arm to tense, and he would often wake with a muscle cramp. He had also come to realize that he had his most vivid dreams lying on his back. In his situation any entertainment was most welcome.

One dream in particular kept resurfacing. In the dream he was a child, sneaking around the Fortress after dark. After checking on his siblings to make sure they were asleep, he snuck out and headed for the main building. The main building had a family room where his parents would talk or read. The building was illuminated by candlelight, so there was darkness and shadows for him to hide in. Slowly, he crept up on his parents. He could see them vividly. He finally came within earshot of their conversation.

"Have you heard from your brother?" his mother asked.

"Not in two weeks," his father answered, putting aside the book he was reading.

"What about the kids?"

"What about them?"

"Will we ever tell them they have cousins?" she asked.

"One day, I suppose."

"I think we should tell them they are not alone."

At that moment in the dream, Michael bolted upright. Sweat had formed on his forehead. His heart was beating faster. In that lucid moment, he realized it was more than a dream. It was a memory.

———

Alexa Wallace tossed and turned fitfully for two hours before falling asleep. Her dinner with Sutter had been more than she had expected. She felt safe with him, as in a sanctuary. She had never had a relationship of this sort, and it was confusing. Alexa's main concern was that she would lose her focus. She understood that if she lost her edge, she would be captured, and her mission would fail.

That night, in her dream, Alexa was being pursued by a man. She quickened her pace, but her tormentor kept gaining on her. She sprinted as fast as possible, yet still he gained. Defensively, Alexa turned around to confront her attacker.

To her shock it was Sutter. She pulled her pistol and put pressure on the trigger. The gun would not fire. Alexa used all her strength on the trigger, but she could not pull it all the way. Her efforts were in vain. Sutter looked at her, tears in his eyes.

In that instant, her alarm clock jolted her awake. Alexa spent the rest of the day unsuccessfully trying to decipher the dream's hidden meaning.

———

Sullivan was accustomed to having very elaborate nightmares. They tended to consume his subconscious. Often they involved natural disasters, such as huge tidal waves or earthquakes. In all of them, Sullivan survived. An expert on dream analysis once told him that this was a good sign. Not the nightmares themselves. They were a sign of high stress levels. The fact that he survived them was good news. It indicated that he was dealing with the stress and that he had the instinct to always come out on top.

This dream was different, however. In it he was back at the FBI Academy as a trainee. His instructor was discussing the survivability of various injuries. It was a lecture that Instructor Bill James, a legend in the FBI, was passionate about.

"So in conclusion the vast majority of injuries are survivable."

The class listened attentively as the instructor summarized the lesson.

Sullivan raised his hand. James pointed at him.

"Which ones aren't survivable?" he said as the class chuckled.

"Clearly, a direct bullet to the skull is instantly lethal. In some cases, however, the skull will divert the bullet and the wound can be survivable, depending on the caliber of the round."

James was using a dummy for demonstration purposes. He continued.

"A direct round to the heart, center mass, is also lethal." He pointed at the dummy's heart.

James drilled into his trainees the importance of willpower in a life-and-death struggle. He focused their training for the one day they would come face-to-face with death. In his mind victory was the only option, even if death was the result.

"Even after being mortally wounded," he lectured, "you have several seconds where you can and *must* act!"

He could see the surprise in the faces of the trainees. Sullivan stared at him, listening intently.

"That's right, Sullivan." He pointed. "Those crucial seconds can give you the time to take your enemy with you."

At that moment, Sullivan awoke abruptly. His sheet was soaked in sweat. He stared at the ceiling for a full minute before finally getting up. He had to lead the team into a lion's den. As much as he dreaded the harm to his friend's careers, he was eager to get the bad news out of the way.

He had a coyote to catch.

TWENTY FIVE

Meetings

Alexa sat across from Warden Robert Underwood, both legs planted on the floor in front of her military style. Her hair was in a bun, her Bureau of Prisons uniform immaculate. Her blue shirt was neatly tucked into her pants, which were crisply pressed. The polish on her boots was so perfect that she could almost see her reflection in them as the light bounced off her left boot. She had spent over an hour polishing them the night before. In her opinion her BOP academy instructors had not sufficiently stressed proper discipline in their attire. Much to her chagrin, they did not enforce clothing etiquette to her standards. She felt that this was another deficiency in their required training. By the same token, this gave her a way to stand out in a positive manner. She wanted to make a good impression on her first day on the job. This was her first opportunity to wear the uniform since she joined the BOP.

Seated to Alexa's right was Captain Wayne Benham, who had greeted her when she first reported for duty. He had given her a brief tour of the facility. Benham had escorted her through the fortress known as the ADX Supermax to the warden's office. He said little during the tour. He appeared to be a man of few words.

During the tour Alexa made mental notes of all that she saw. She observed the difficulty of navigating within the facility. Checkpoints were numerous. Cameras were as ubiquitous as they were in casinos.

No corner of the prison had a blind spot. Thankfully, she thought, her plan required guile and not brawn.

As Underwood looked through some papers, he finally found the folder he had been looking for, and he turned his attention to Alexa.

"Ms. Fisher," he started, "I've read your file."

"Yes, sir." She answered without smiling.

"Captain Sanders, back at headquarters, thinks very highly of you." He held the folder in his hand.

"Thank you, sir."

"My concern, quite frankly, is that you have no experience in a penitentiary."

He looked at her, one eye arched skeptically.

"I know, sir, but I learn quickly." She sat at attention.

"I'm counting on that, Ms. Fisher."

"I won't let you down."

Underwood looked at his captain.

"Captain Benham will be monitoring your progress," he said.

"I've already told her she has big shoes to fill," Benham jumped in.

Alexa detected the tinge of sadness that crept into their faces.

"Yes, sir," she added respectfully.

"You will start on a rotation," Underwood said.

"Excuse me, sir. What is a rotation?"

"That means you will perform every function in the prison at least once before you are permanently assigned a post." Benham answered for the warden.

"Yes, sir."

The warden's body language signaled that the meeting was ending. He looked at the clock on his wall for a moment. Similarly, Benham checked the time as well. Their stomachs were telling them that is was lunchtime.

"Welcome to ADX Supermax, Ms. Fisher," Underwood finally said. He got up from his seat and extended his hand.

Alexa got up and shook his hand firmly.

"Thank you again, sir."

As they left the warden's office, Alexa could not suppress a slight smile. Her rotational duties were the best possible news. She knew she would soon be seeing her brother.

———

The SAC conference room on the sixth floor of the Boston FBI office is reserved for the most important meetings. The special agent in charge meets with his executive staff on a weekly basis in the room. Its large glass windows overlook Boston's iconic City Hall Plaza. The Boston mayor's office window is within view as it is on the opposite end of the plaza.

A somber, hushed mood enveloped the conference room as SAC Whitworth sat at the end of the long table. The SAC's assistants, Rand and Billings, sat on either side of him. Also seated next to them was Supervisory Special Agent Bill Walker, from FBI HQ. He had been desperate to stop Sullivan and his team since the Coyote investigation had been transferred to him.

In the hallway, outside the conference-room door, former ASAC Gibbons stood watch gleefully. Seeing Sullivan taken to the woodshed made him ecstatic. He smiled as Sullivan approached, hoping to catch his eye. To his dismay Sullivan passed him as if he was nonexistent.

Sullivan entered the room, followed by the team. As he walked in, he thought for a moment that he was entering a star chamber. His judges were seated like kings presiding over their subjects.

Sullivan sat down, Conrad at his side and then O'Keefe. On the other side of the table sat Riley, Rogers, and Goldwein. Goldwein had recovered completely after a night of rest.

Wheeler, wearing a patch on one eye, was the last to enter. He had been told he need not be there, given he was still on medical leave, but he insisted on attending. He was still pale and weak. Sullivan had counseled him into skipping the meeting, but he was adamant.

Whitworth opened the meeting.

"First of all, I'm here to make an announcement. This is not a give-and-take meeting." He looked at them sternly, one at a time.

"With the exception of O'Keefe," he said dramatically, "you are all on suspension until further notice. The Office of Professional Responsibility has opened an investigation into your antics."

The team said nothing. O'Keefe shook her head, objecting.

"But, sir—" O'Keefe pleaded.

"I don't have any evidence, at this time, that you were involved in this unauthorized operation in Virginia." He intoned gravely at O'Keefe.

O'Keefe desperately wanted the same punishment as her friends, but Conrad grabbed her arm. Likewise, Sullivan gave her a look that screamed, "Don't argue."

"You have all participated in an unauthorized investigation that led to injuries."

"Mr. Whitworth, I would like to take full responsibility. Please don't take it out on them. They are all exemplary employees," Sullivan said, looking around the table.

"I'm sorry, Sullivan, not this time. Everyone has to take some responsibility." His tone indicated that there was no wavering from this position.

"Wheeler," he continued, "your suspension will commence once you have recovered. Until then, you will remain on medical leave."

The team looked at their judges with resignation. O'Keefe, who was not suspended, was the most upset.

"I have suspension letters for each of you. I will call you up. You will then leave your weapons and badges on the table before you leave," he pronounced, ending the tribunal.

"Carlos A. Sullivan," he started.

Sullivan retrieved his letter and did as instructed.

"James P. Conrad," he read next and then continued with the others.

After they were done, they met in the hallway and headed for the exit.

As they were leaving, Conrad cornered Goldwein. "Hey, looks like you will have time for that vacation after all."

"Ha ha," she answered.

Looking at their leader, Goldwein asked, "How's that champagne tasting, Sully?"

He shook his head and headed for the exits. The team followed close behind. As they waited for the elevators, they paused at the FBI's *Ten Most Wanted* posters. It was the first thing visitors to the Boston FBI office saw when they arrived. They couldn't help but review the Alexa Wallace sketch. Conrad pointed his index finger at her forehead as if he held a pistol.

The team chuckled as the elevator arrived.

The team descended to the first floor and out into the brisk May air. They crossed the street onto City Hall Plaza, casually walking with no real purpose. None of them wanted to leave each other. They were all in the same leaky boat.

They all finally took a seat on a U-shaped wooden bench on the plaza. O'Keefe broke the silence.

"I feel so bad that I was spared," she said, a tear welling in her eye.

"Don't be silly, Trish," Sullivan said. "We need someone on the inside."

"Inside?" Goldwein was incredulous. "You plan on going forward?"

"Of course," he answered. "You don't drop out of a marathon at mile twenty-five."

"Oh my God, you are crazy."

"We did come very close," Conrad said.

They all shook their heads in agreement. Goldwein was still skeptical, but she admired their dedication. She felt part of something special.

"But we don't even have weapons, Sully. You saw how dangerous she is."

"That won't be a problem." He smiled.

Conrad looked at him and chuckled.

TWENTY SIX

Brothers to the Rescue

Twenty-five miles west of Boston, it was an unseasonably warm, cloudless day. A family of geese waddled through an opening in a field and onto the far end of a five hundred-foot airstrip. They were crossing from one side to the other in search of food. Next to the airstrip was a small abandoned house. A decrepit wooden sign outside of the house jokingly boasted, *Marlborough International Airport*.

Sullivan had parked his car perpendicular to the airstrip, and he sat on the hood, looking skyward. Conrad remained in the front passenger seat, reading a magazine. Riley and Goldwein got out of the backseat and stood next to Sullivan.

"What exactly are we doing here?" Goldwein asked.

"Meeting someone."

"Who?" she asked impatiently.

"You will see soon enough."

Sullivan scanned the sky more intensely as he heard the low-droning sound of an approaching aircraft.

A white Cessna turboprop banked toward the airstrip, positioning itself for a landing. Sullivan rapped on the hood of the car, getting Conrad's attention. He got out and joined the team as they watched the plane touch down and then slowly ramble over to where they were parked.

After the Coyote attacks, brothers Jorge and Miguel had several publicity tours. Their helicopter exploits during the incident made them minicelebrities. Likewise, Jim McDougal, the owner of Capitol Area Helo Tours, made some promotional videos highlighting his role in furnishing the helicopters that were used to track and capture Michael Wallace. It was only natural for them to collaborate in a new business venture. McDougal expanded his business to include small aircraft and hired Miguel and Jorge as pilots in that endeavor.

The plane's rotor blades finally stopped spinning, and the pilots bounded out of the plane.

"My friends," they gushed, each one hugging Sullivan and then Conrad.

"It's been too long," Sullivan declared.

"Yes, we stay busy," Jorge said in his thick Colombian accent.

"*Cómo están?*" Miguel asked them.

"We are well, Miguel, and thank you for coming."

"Always, Sully." They nodded.

"I want you to meet Agents Riley and Goldwein." Sullivan introduced the brothers.

They shook hands eagerly.

"I've heard of you guys," Riley stated.

"Gracias," Jorge replied.

"Do you have the items?" Sullivan asked.

"Of course."

Miguel then walked to the plane, returning a minute later with a duffel bag.

Goldwein's eyes widened as Miguel started pulling weapons out of the bag. Sullivan looked on approvingly as Conrad handled each one and put them on the hood of the car.

"Four Smith & Wesson nine-millimeter pistols with two full magazines each." Conrad counted. "One Remington twelve-gauge shotgun and an M-four carbine."

"I'll take the shotgun," Riley called out.

Conrad tossed it to him, and he cradled it with both hands.

He handed each member one of the pistols. Conrad then took the carbine and placed it in the trunk.

Miguel and Jorge, realizing their job was done, bade them all farewell and got back in their plane. The rotor whizzed to life, and they turned the plane around, facing the open airstrip. They watched silently as the Cessna roared into the open sky.

Goldwein then put voice to what they were all thinking.

"Now all we have to do is find her."

They got in their car, and Sullivan drove them off the field.

TWENTY SEVEN

Acceptance

Alexa's first assignment was in the prison's command center. The command center is the facility's central nervous system. It keeps everything in check. All cameras are monitored from the center. Passage through the Supermax's hallways is strictly controlled from this unit. All persons seeking access to a passageway must press an intercom. The signal is received in the center. The officer on duty views the requesting employee through the system's cameras. Once visual confirmation is made, the doors are opened.

Captain Benham had introduced her to the duty sergeant, Will Hesser, with a word of advice. "Listen and learn, Fisher," he declared before walking away.

Hesser was a twenty-year veteran of the Bureau of Prisons. Gravity had not been kind to the sergeant over the years, as his large belly protruded over his belt. He was fond of telling everyone who would listen how he planned on retiring to Florida. He was tired of the cold and the snow. As he watched Alexa reviewing the log books he had shown her, he thought that she reminded him of his own daughter. Ordinarily, the thought of training a new officer did not appeal to him. In this instance, however, he decided to take an interest.

"Fisher, will you be attending Captain Benham's party?"

The question hung in the air for a moment. The captain had invited Alexa, but she was disinclined to accept. The party was meant to be a celebration of Wesley Hughes's life—the equivalent of an Irish wake. She was concerned about getting too close to her coworkers.

"I don't think so," she finally answered.

"You really should go," he counseled her.

"I never knew him."

"It doesn't matter. If you want to be accepted around here, you will go."

She pondered his words quietly.

"We are like a family here," he stressed.

"Maybe you are right."

"I am, believe me."

"OK, then." She decided to go out of concern that her absence might raise eyebrows. She wanted to be trusted, as her plans depended on it.

"Do you have a boyfriend?" the sergeant asked her.

The question took her by surprise. "Why?"

"You are the only young female working in here in case you hadn't noticed."

Hesser had heard the buzz from the young officers at the facility. Word had spread quickly that Hughes's replacement was an attractive young female.

Alexa thought about Hesser's advice and the implications it entailed. The last thing she needed was to be pursued romantically at work. It would lead to resentments from her colleagues if she rejected their advances. Then she thought of Sutter.

"Yes," she said, "I do. And I will be taking him to the party."

Sutter would once again prove to be useful, she thought to herself.

———

At Sullivan's suggestion Goldwein decided to return to the NSA. She still had her access badge. If she could access the NSA database once more, she might be able to see what other sites Alexa Wallace had been visiting from the Reston computers. It was natural to assume that such a review might allow her to connect more dots.

Still, she had doubts about the unscrupulous manner by which she had gained access. Prior to leaving for Fort Meade, she had stopped by Trish O'Keefe's cubicle for a discussion. As she approached the NSA's main gate, she recalled the conversation.

"Trish," she asked, leaning over her desk, "what exactly did you find out about Mr. Berlin?"

"Your conscience is bothering you?" Trish stared at Suzanne, her elbow on the desk, a fist under her chin.

"Yeah, I guess."

"So you want me to tell you he's a monster. Will that make you feel better?"

"I don't know, maybe."

"If you must know, he's using the Internet to solicit sex online. It's called prostitution."

"I know what it is. Is that all?"

"He has a top-secret clearance, Suzanne."

Her words hung in the quiet room for a moment.

"Yeah, I know. He's compromising his position—"

"And he's gone into deep debt doing it," O'Keefe interrupted.

"I get it. I get it."

The memory was fresh as she approached the security gate. This was the first check in the process. During a recent security incident, two men driving an SUV had attempted to ram through security. A shooting ensued, and one of the attackers was killed. As a result security was doubled at the main gate, which she noticed immediately. She stopped at the guard station, displayed her badge, and was waved forward.

Easy enough, she thought. She found a parking spot in the massive parking lot and walked into the employee entrance. This was the second security step.

Goldwein swiped her access badge at the entrance and walked in unmolested. However, her entry triggered a silent alarm. She took the elevator and made her way to the cubicle she had been assigned. To her surprise it was exactly as she had left it.

She turned on her computer, waiting as it booted up. This process usually took about sixty seconds. As she waited, she could hear the shuffle of feet approaching. She turned and saw two burly security officers approaching, escorting Director Berlin to her station. From their expressions she knew it was not a welcoming committee.

"Come with us, Ms. Goldwein," Berlin said sternly.

They walked her back the way she had entered, the officers flanking her as they did so. Berlin, in particular, had a dour expression on his face. When they reached the lobby, Berlin pointed at her.

"We were informed of your suspension," he admonished her.

"I see," she answered meekly.

"You are not to return here ever again."

With one motion, Berlin reached down to her badge and pulled it off the blouse she had clipped it to. He looked at her one last time. "Ever."

Goldewin smiled slightly as she left the building, glad for this entire episode to be over.

Her acceptance at the NSA had come to an abrupt conclusion.

TWENTY EIGHT

Preparations

Alexa drove her blue Ford F-150 pickup truck onto the lot of *Jim's Auto Body* in Colorado Springs, which specialized in painting and repairs. She had already affixed her new Colorado license plates to the vehicle. She wanted to blend in as smoothly as possible. Standing outside her vehicle for only a moment, a worker, dressed in paint-speckled jeans, walked out to greet her.

"Hello there," he said, smiling. "I'm Billy."

"I'm Amanda."

"What can I do for you?"

She looked at her Ford and pointed at it. "Can you paint it red for me?"

"Are you sure, miss? That is a good paint job you have there," he asked, puzzled.

"Yeah, I'm just not happy with this color." She shrugged.

"How red do you want it?"

"As bright red as you can make it." She smiled.

"Well, sure."

"How long will it take?"

"To do a good job, we need a full day." He cleaned his hands on his jeans as he talked.

"Great."

"Come into our office, and we will schedule you." He waved toward the office.

———

Sullivan sat at the end of his motel bed and flipped through his television channels in a continuous loop, never settling on any particular program. His mind was working in overdrive. In the room next door, Riley was taking a shower. His thoughts were on his girlfriend, who was upset that he was leaving town. He would be missing her birthday. He would make it up to her, he thought to himself.

After several hours of driving, they were both tired and needed a rest. They settled into a cheap motel in Illinois, just west of Chicago. Sullivan turned the TV's volume down when he heard his cell phone buzzing. He could see from the caller ID that it was his associate from the Denver office.

"Hey there, Jamie," Sullivan began. "Thanks for calling me back."

"No problem," he said. "How are you holding up?"

Sullivan knew that his team's woes were well known throughout the entire Bureau. Such an event could not be kept a secret.

"I'm fine, Jamie. Thanks for asking."

"What can I do for you?"

"Do you know if Warden Underwood knows about the suspensions?"

"I'm not sure, but I doubt it."

"I see."

"They are pretty isolated out there, and I know I haven't told him."

"Why do you ask?" he inquired.

"I'm headed your way again."

"Seriously?" Banks was surprised.

"Yeah, I'm going to take another crack at Michael Wallace. I want to make sure I can get access to him again."

"Well, I guess you won't know for sure until you get there," Banks joked.

"I guess you're right about that." He smiled.

"Good luck, Sully," Banks said before hanging up.

Sullivan turned the TV off and got ready for bed. He and Riley had a lot of driving still ahead of them.

———

Conrad sat across from Detective Dominguez at the Dunkin' Donuts located in front of the Boston FBI office, next to the Government Center T Station. Curiously, it was located only a few feet from a Starbucks. Conrad was not a coffee drinker, so he never understood the Starbucks versus Dunkin' debate. To him coffee was just coffee. Yet he knew that like many die-hard Bostonians, Detective Dominguez was decidedly anti-Starbucks. He would not ever be caught drinking anything but Dunkin' Donuts coffee. It was on that basis that he selected their meeting venue.

Conrad watched silently as Dominguez added sugar to his cup and then swirled his warm beverage. As he did this, Dominguez looked out the window, scrutinizing every passerby as would be expected of an experienced detective. He usually started by checking out their footwear, and then he made his way up. Each inspection took only a few seconds. After each evaluation Dominguez would pass judgment—good guy or bad guy—in his mental ledger.

Conrad knew to wait until his friend was ready before bringing up business. His assignment was to stay in Boston and help Dominguez find their elusive witnesses. He had expected Dominguez to have found them by now. When he sensed the time was right, he leaned over in his seat.

"Do you have any idea where they could be?"

"None."

"Do you think Sonny's mother is covering for him?"

"No way. I've established a good rapport with her," Dominguez said, sipping his coffee.

"Well, we could really use a break in this case," Conrad said, wistfully.

"Jimmy, I'm convinced she will tell me where her son is once she knows."

"Then we'll do what we do best." Conrad chuckled.

"Absolutely." Dominguez smiled back.

A light rain pelted central Colorado. The raindrops bounced off Alexa's truck as she pulled into a small strip mall. She parked and looked about, annoyed. She could not find the business she was looking for, despite the fact that she was at the correct address. She noticed that one of the businesses did not have a sign, but she could see that there was someone inside.

She walked in and greeted a slender man in his thirties reading a book behind a counter. He looked mildly irritated that he was interrupted.

"May I help you?"

"Yes, is this *Morrissey's Medical Supply and Equipment?*" she asked.

"Yes it is."

"Why is there no sign outside?" She pointed to the door.

"We don't have many walk-ins. Most of our business is to local hospitals and clinics," he explained.

"I see. Well, perhaps you can help me."

"I will try."

Alexa handed him a list from her pocket.

"Let's see." He folded the list open. "You need four syringes, medical bandages, intravenous lines and bags, saline solution, an oxygen tank with face mask, and a blood-pressure bulb and gauge."

He looked at his young client with curiosity. "Are you going to open a clinic?"

"Don't forget the thermometer," she said as he scrutinized the list again.

"Ah, yes."

"Well, do you have those items?"

She had one hand on her hip. Alexa was not in the mood for an attitude.

"Sure," he said finally, "but it won't be cheap."

"No problem," she said. "I'll be paying in cash."

TWENTY NINE

Party

Alexa watched from her apartment window for any sign of David. After much fretting about what to wear, she had settled on a yellow sundress. She wore a light sweater over it as it was still prone to colder weather at night. She thought back to the moment she had invited him to the party and the glee in his voice as he accepted. She realized the party was more important to David than it was to her. It was a signal to him that she was making their relationship official.

Despite her trust in him, she had still not invited him into her apartment. It was a barrier she was still not ready to cross. She told him that she would watch for his car and come out to meet him. When he finally pulled into the parking lot, he flashed his lights, signaling his arrival. How cute, she thought.

On their drive to Florence, Alexa once more went over the protocols.

"Please remember not to mention my asthma," she said.

"To be honest, Amanda, I would never know you had asthma."

He was too enamored with her to doubt her story, despite the fact that her supposed malady made such a miraculous remission.

"And don't forget about my mom, in case that comes up."

"Don't worry, I've got this."

She reached over and brushed the back of his head affectionately.

"I know, Dave. I know."

—

Captain Benham and his wife, Wendy, greeted every person as each one arrived for their party. Behind them were Hughes's parents, Samuel and Victoria, who were the guests of honor. They also welcomed the visitors, most of whom had been friends or colleagues of their son. In the backyard, Wesley's brother Adam played with Tucker, who was grateful for the company.

As people streamed in, they stood at their open front door, shaking hands and patting their guests on the back with affection. On a small table in the foyer, a picture of Wesley Hughes in his uniform was displayed. The Benhams were the picture of cordiality. In Florence they were well known for their hospitality and thoughtfulness.

Parking spaces were at a premium. Cars were lined up as far as two blocks away from the house. Many of Benham's neighbors were BOP employees and were also in attendance. Benham had only known Alexa for a short time, but he smiled when he saw her approaching. He was pleased that their newest officer decided to attend the party. It was a sign of respect. He greeted her and Sutter enthusiastically.

"Welcome, Amanda," he said. "Make yourself at home."

Alexa poured herself some ginger ale from the counter and found a beer for David. They held hands as they walked about the house reviewing the Benhams' family pictures. She wanted to make sure everybody knew she was in a relationship. Almost immediately they bumped into Sergeant Hesser, who nodded approvingly.

"Good to see you here, Fisher." He smiled.

"I'm glad I came, Sergeant."

"You must be the boyfriend," he said.

"Dave Sutter," he replied, "at your service."

They shook hands. Hesser put his arm around Sutter's shoulder.

"You should see the game room in the basement," he said to Sutter.

Dave looked at Alexa for guidance.

"Go ahead. Have fun," she said.

As they walked away, she could hear Hesser talking nonstop.

"They have a pool table, or we could play darts. You play pool, don't you, Dave…"

Once they were out of sight, Alexa plopped herself on one of the living-room couches. Watching the guests chatting among themselves, her thoughts turned to all the things she still needed to do. As she reviewed her mental checklist, a nearby conversation suddenly caught her attention. Her ears perked up as she focused on the conversation behind her.

"So how long have you been a doctor?" a female guest asked.

"Well, almost fifteen years."

"Is this your first time working at a prison?"

"Yes, actually. I'm finding it quite interesting."

As they spoke, Alexa subtly rose from her seat and walked to the side of the couch. From there she scrutinized every detail of the doctor. Although she was new to the prison, she had already heard the jokes about the doctor's lack of skills. She watched him closely, taking note of his height, weight, and attire. They were oblivious to her presence. When their conversation ended and the doctor finally drifted off, Alexa walked over to the woman who had been talking to him.

"Excuse me. Who was that you were talking to?"

"That was Doctor Julius Winchester," she answered. "He works at the prison infirmary,"

Alexa nodded her head silently.

"Would you like me to introduce you?" she asked helpfully.

"Oh, no, thank you. I had him confused with someone else."

Alexa then turned and watched as the doctor made his way through the room. She eyed him carefully as he poured himself another glass of Scotch. He plopped two ice cubes into the glass before taking another swig. As he did so, Alexa noticed the slight, almost imperceptible tremble of his hand.

———

Alexa needed an ice refill for her ginger ale, so she headed to the kitchen. She used the tongs in an ice bucket to chill her drink. As she did so, she looked to her right through the sliding glass door which led to the yard. As she did, Tucker looked straight back at her and started growling. From the yard he leapt onto the back porch and stopped just at the glass. He was now barking uncontrollably, his front paws banging violently against the door. Alexa glared at the dog, her teeth clenched defiantly.

Confused, Adam Hughes quickly grabbed Tucker's collar and dragged him away from the door. Alexa, not wanting to exacerbate the situation, quickly left the kitchen. It would take another thirty minutes to calm Tucker. The incident convinced Alexa that it was time to leave.

She walked down to the basement in search of her date. She had accomplished what she wanted and was ready for the night to end. When she reached the basement, what she saw brought a smile to her face. Dave was engaged in an animated conversation with several of her male colleagues. In their short time at the party, it seemed Dave had gotten to know her coworkers better than she did. She enjoyed watching him engage her peers so naturally.

The image also gave her pause, however. She was starting to have feelings for Dave. She wondered, would she be able to put that aside to fulfill her mission? Perhaps Dave would not be a factor in her ultimate plans after all. If not then she would spare him, she decided. Otherwise, his fate was sealed. As she considered this, Dave saw her and called her over.

"Hey, guys," she greeted her colleagues.

"You're ready to leave?" he asked.

"If you are."

"All right," he said.

Dave shook hands with his new friends. They had already invited him to another party.

As they were walking to the door, Sergeant Hesser caught her leaving and intercepted them to say good-bye.

"See you tomorrow, Sergeant," She said.

"Yeah, tomorrow should be interesting."

"What's up tomorrow?" She furrowed her brow.

"The FBI is in town."

Her heart skipped a beat.

"Why?"

"They are here to interview Inmate Wallace."

"Oh, I see," she said, trying to appear calm.

"Well, be safe, and it was nice to meet you," he said, looking at Sutter.

As they left, Sutter wondered if he had made a good impression. Alexa's thoughts, on the other hand, were decidedly more serious.

⁓

THIRTY

Timing

Alexa sat uncomfortably in her chair in the prison's command center. Working nearby, other officers chatted either among themselves or on the telephone. Cell phones were not allowed in the facility, but the command center had several hard lines. Usually, Alexa could block out the static. Today, however, their noise was irritating her.

Sergeant Hesser munched on a donut as he usually did in the morning. Periodically, Alexa monitored the cameras focused on the parking lot. In particular, the small visitor-parking section. She knew that Agent Sullivan would surely recognize her instantly. She also knew that he would come past the command center on his way to the visitors' conference room. The glass windows offered a perfect view into the center. She had to find a way to excuse herself.

That morning, she had walked past the visitor-parking section on her way into the facility. Using her watch, she timed how long it took to walk from the parking lot into the facility. Ninety seconds. Then she calculated their stop at reception. Signing in, storing weapons, and then waiting for an escort probably took five minutes, at least. Then she timed the walk from reception to the command center. Three minutes.

To be safe, she estimated she needed no less than ten minutes away from her post. She had briefly considered calling in sick, except that she had been seen at the party and she was fine. In addition she was new and under probation. She could use the bathroom, but for ten minutes? There was a unisex bathroom in the command center. Everyone could see her enter.

Alexa looked at the clock on the far side of the command center. It was already nine o'clock. Surely, the agents would be there soon. She knew they were in town, and there was nothing to do in Florence. Her eyes went from the clock to the monitor. Finally, she saw them. A dark-green Chevy Impala pulled into one of the four spaces reserved for visitors.

Her concentration now completely on the screen, she watched Sullivan and Riley get out of their car. She recognized the driver immediately. It was Sullivan. The passenger she remembered as the man outside the library. On this occasion he had no earpiece.

She checked her watch as they approached the building. From another camera she saw them entering the reception area.

"Sarge." She looked over at Hesser. "I'm not feeling well."

"Is everything OK?"

She walked over to him and whispered, "Female issues, Sarge."

His eyes widened. "Oh, yes, take whatever time you need."

Hesser had never had this issue come up before. Alexa walked into the bathroom and locked the door. It was 9:08 a.m.

———

Officer Roach was reading a magazine and sipping his coffee when Sullivan and Riley walked into the reception area.

"You must be the FBI agents," he declared, putting his cup on the desk.

"Is it that obvious?" Sullivan smiled.

"We were expecting you. Captain Benham will be escorting you. I'll let him know you're here."

"Great," Riley said.

Roach reached for the visitors' ledger.

"I just need to see your IDs."

Sullivan and Riley looked at each other, stunned. They had failed to consider they had no FBI credentials. He started to pat his jacket down, trying to quickly think of an excuse. Just at that moment, Warden Underwood appeared, seemingly out of nowhere.

"Hey there! I'm glad I caught you. I was running a little late today," he said apologetically.

Sullivan had left the warden a message indicating their intentions. When he had not heard back, he had started to worry that they would not be well received. Now, those fears dissipated instantly.

They exchanged handshakes. The warden then waited while they signed the ledger. Officer Roach then took Sullivan and Riley into a small room. One wall was covered with lockboxes. They placed their weapons and cell phones in one of the boxes. Sullivan pocketed the key.

When they came back out to reception, the warden was waiting.

"How is Banks doing?" he asked.

"Well, I just spoke to him two days ago."

The warden then proceeded to tell a story about a golf outing he once had with Banks. Underwood was animated as he talked about how Banks was a notorious golf cheater. They listened patiently, grateful that they had just gotten very lucky.

The clock on the wall read 9:14 a.m.

—

Alexa waited in the bathroom ticking off the seconds in her head. Every so often, she put her ear to the door to see if she could hear anything. Yet the steel door frustrated those attempts. She was so close to her brother. She could not be stopped now, she thought.

As her watch signaled it was 9:18 a.m., she heard someone pull on the door from the other side. It was locked. It's only been ten minutes, she thought. Should she come out? One of her colleagues was now waiting on the other side of the door.

—

Sullivan and Riley noticed the warden seemed unusually gregarious. On their previous visit, he had seemed much more reserved. Perhaps as a warden he needed to project a certain image with first-time visitors. Now that he was meeting them for a second time, he had lowered his guard.

As they walked toward the command center, they chatted freely.

"Warden, does he receive any mail?" Riley asked.

"Well, typically inmates here can receive mail."

"Typically?" Sullivan replied.

"Yes, in Wallace's case, however, the court has imposed what are called special administrative measures, known as SAMs."

"I see," Riley answered. His face and tone signaled that he was inquiring further.

"Those are measures to limit a prisoner's rights to outside contacts. In terrorism cases they are imposed to prevent the inmate from conspiring with confederates."

"I've heard of SAMs before." Sullivan nodded.

"They will most likely stay in place until you catch his sister."

Underwood stopped in the corridor for a moment and looked at his visitors.

"You *do* plan on catching her." He smiled.

"We sure hope so."

They all laughed as they approached the command center. The clock on the wall read 9:20 a.m.

———

Alexa looked at her watch again, calculating her move. It was now 9:20 a.m.; twelve minutes had elapsed. Surely they must have passed through by now. She was also worried that the sergeant might try checking on her condition, drawing attention to her. What if he did this as the agents were passing by? Her mind was racing.

She reached for the doorknob.

———

Sullivan looked into the command center, scanning the room. The room was well lit and had a tactical feel. He could easily envision the same room inside a modern naval warship. Sergeant Hesser approached from the other side of the glass. Sullivan noticed another officer in the rear, waiting outside a door labeled *Bathroom.*

"Coming through, Sarge," Underwood declared.

Hesser pressed the command button, and their door slid open slowly, allowing them passage to the next section of the facility and onto the visitors' area.

As the door opened and they passed through, the clock read 9:21 a.m.

—

Alexa slowly opened the door. As she did so, she could see the warden and his visitors walking away from the command center. Her colleague quickly went into the bathroom as she held her breath. If they turned back, she would be seen. She watched them closely as they got farther and farther away. Finally, they turned a corner.

Alexa took her seat in front of a monitor. From there she would finally be able to see her brother.

THIRTY ONE

Round Two

Having narrowly dodged a bullet, Alexa returned to her monitoring station. She was animated as she checked the master sheet of cameras. This would be her first opportunity to see her brother since his captivity. She quickly found the camera that was trained to tier-two passageway from cells one through fifteen. As she clicked the mouse over that camera icon, she held her breath. The black-and-white image was clear. Three of her fellow corrections officers were in the hallway outside of cell thirteen. They were waiting for her brother to come to the door. She watched as one of the guards leaned into the opening in the door with his handcuffs.

A moment later her brother appeared on the screen, looking straight ahead as another guard placed leg shackles on him. It was a surreal experience for her. She touched the screen, caressing Michael's head, just as they started to walk down the hallway. So close, she thought.

"Fisher," she heard, startled. She turned to see the sergeant headed in her direction.

"Are you OK?" he asked, walking closer to her.

She quickly flicked the mouse to another camera.

"Yes, Sarge. I'm feeling better, thank you."

"Would you like to take leave?" He seemed genuinely concerned.

"Oh, no, absolutely not," she said without hesitation. She was looking forward to watching her brother, even if through a camera. Alexa would not miss the opportunity for anything.

"All right," he said, walking away.

Once he was far enough away, Alexa swiveled her chair back to her monitor.

———

As Sullivan and Riley watched, the guards removed Wallace's restraints. One of them looked over at Sullivan before they walked out.

"We'll be outside," he said with a matter-of-fact tone.

Sullivan nodded silently. He then turned his attention to Wallace, who sat across from them, his elbows on the table, hands clasped together. Sullivan knew that in this situation, whoever spoke first would be at a psychological disadvantage. He wanted to retain control, so he said nothing. Similarly, Wallace simply stared at them. Sullivan stared back, taking a moment to glance at Wallace's watch. It was his way of telling Wallace that he owed them.

"You're back," Wallace finally said.

"I told you we would be."

"Well, I haven't had an opportunity to write anything for you yet."

"Too busy?"

"You're a funny guy." Wallace smirked.

"That's a shame because I was prepared to deliver a letter to your sister for you." Sullivan shrugged, looking at Wallace and then Riley who nodded in silent agreement.

"I just don't believe you." Wallace crossed his arms.

"Why would I lie about that?" Sullivan leaned back.

"You're trying to get in my head."

"To what end?"

"Maybe you get some perverted satisfaction from screwing with me."

Sullivan gave an exasperated gesture with his arms and then looked at Riley.

"Maybe we're wasting our time," Riley finally spoke.

The comment struck a nerve with Wallace, as it was intended. While he was extremely dubious regarding what he was hearing, it was infinitely more interesting than languishing in his cell. That was mind-numbing. He did not want to admit it, but he actually found the interaction entertaining.

"Why don't you give me some proof, like her mug shot?" Wallace leaned forward.

"That's against the rules as you know. I've already cashed in a huge favor to get you that watch," Sullivan said seriously.

Wallace nodded and smiled, impressed with Sullivan's cleverness. Not only did he give him a reason for not offering proof, but he was reminding him of the watch.

"Well played, Agent Sullivan."

"This isn't personal for me, to be clear."

Wallace glared at them with a mix of frustration and anger. He leaned as far forward as possible without actually standing up.

"It's not personal for me either, Agent Sullivan. But if I ever get a chance, I want you to know that I wouldn't hesitate to kill you." His voice was menacing and dry.

Sullivan's reaction surprised him. He smiled and looked back at him. "I don't know, Mr. Wallace. I think if you tried to kill me I *would* take that personally."

———

Alexa watched in rapt attention. The camera in the visitors' room gave her a clear view of the action, but no sound. Still, she could assess her brother's body language. His mood seemed to oscillate between anger and entertainment. One moment he was smiling; the next he seemed threatening. The meeting had entered its third hour. She watched as they took a lunch break. The warden had arranged for meals to be sent to them. She looked at the clock on the wall. It was 12:22 p.m. She considered that if the meeting concluded before her shift ended at three, she would need another escape. The agents would once more pass by the command center on their way out.

She looked around the command center and saw that nobody was paying her any attention. Two officers talked on hard lines. The sergeant was on the computer, probably playing a game of solitaire, as she had spied him doing earlier. She pulled a turkey sandwich from her brown-bag lunch and started eating as she continued to watch her brother's battle of wits with her pursuers.

———

For almost half an hour, Wallace sat silently, his arms crossed, leaning back slightly on his metal stool, which was welded to the floor. He looked past Sullivan and Riley through the glass window and the outside hallway. There, he saw the three corrections officers chatting among themselves. He knew they would be summoned the minute his interrogators got bored with him. He dreaded the thought of going back to his cage. His mind was split between his deadening boredom and his pride. He debated what to do as he watched Sullivan pass Riley a note.

"I have to admit I was skeptical when you said they wouldn't take the watch," he finally spoke again.

"I gave you my word."

"So you promise you will deliver her a letter for me?"

"I will."

"And you won't read it?" he asked suspiciously.

"I won't."

"What do you get out of it?"

"A continued dialogue with you. I told you that's all I'm asking for."

Wallace scrutinized Sullivan for almost a minute, evaluating his interrogator.

"All right then. I will take you up on it."

Sullivan looked at Riley, who pulled out two folded pieces of white paper and an envelope from his jacket. He then pulled out a pen from another pocket. He reached over and put them before Wallace.

"Here you go," Riley said.

For the next three hours, Wallace took pen to paper. He would write for a minute or so and then stop for a time, seemingly in thought. Sullivan and Riley waited patiently, wondering if this strategy would bear any fruit. Riley knew Sullivan was convinced that a letter from Wallace to his sister could have important clues. He himself was not so certain. Nevertheless, he agreed with Sullivan that it was worth a shot.

———

From her perch in the command center, Alexa watched the interview periodically. Her duties took her away from the screen, but she returned to the show as often as possible. She looked at the command-center clock with a mix of relief and disappointment. Her shift was ending. While it meant she would leave the facility before the agents passed by again, she was upset she would have to leave her brother. As she gathered her belongings to leave, the sergeant called to her. She dutifully walked to his desk.

"Fisher, I'm going to miss you, but tomorrow you start a new assignment." He stroked his chin as he spoke. He spoke from behind a desktop computer that partially blocked his view of her.

"Where will I be assigned?" she asked.

"You will be interacting with the inmates. You're being rotated as part of your training."

"What will I be doing?"

"Inmate cell checks and food service," he replied dryly.

"Sorry for asking, but how long will I have that assignment?

"Two days, and then you will be on perimeter duty."

Finally, she thought, direct contact with her brother. Alexa quickly did the math in her head. Her brother would be free in seventy-two hours. She smiled at her boss.

"That's great, Sarge. Thanks for everything. I've learned a lot here." She reached for her bag.

"Have a good evening," he said, turning back to his game of computer solitaire.

As she walked out of the facility, she considered how much she still had to accomplish. Her operational time line had just narrowed.

———

Later that evening Sullivan and Riley convened in the lobby bar of their hotel. They were thirsty and hungry after their full day at the Supermax. After they settled into their bar stools and ordered their first round of drinks, Riley pulled out the envelope Wallace had sealed. On the front he had written, "*Alexa.*"

"How about a drum roll?" Riley smiled.

"What's your bet?"

"I'm not sure. I'd say fifty-fifty. He did spend a lot of time on it."

"Well, open it, and let's see," Sullivan said, taking a sip of beer.

Riley used a pen to rip the envelope open at the top. He slowly pulled out the folded letter, which he could see had writing on both sides. He laughed as he read the contents. He passed the note to Sullivan. In cursive writing Wallace had written the word "*liar*" over and over again. It covered both pages, front and back.

Sullivan chuckled at the sight.

"It doesn't matter. Now we can really break him."

"How so?" Riley asked.

"Wouldn't you say he has to have *some* doubt as to whether we're being honest?"

"Yeah, I'd say so," Riley replied.

"So in two days we go back and tell him we delivered the letter. We give no hint that we've read it."

"So he will be tormented"—Riley smiled—"thinking he blew his only chance to communicate with her."

"Exactly." Sullivan laughed. "It will be killing him."

"I think he's right. You are enjoying screwing with him."

"It's the least we can do after what they've done, Riley."

"I'll drink to that."

They clinked their glasses in a toast.

"To Fuller," they said in unison.

THIRTY TWO

Seventy-Two Hours

Alexa pulled out of the Supermax parking lot with a renewed focus. The first thing she did was reset her trip odometer to zero. She then drove exactly fifteen miles on Route 50 east and slowed down on the heavily forested road. She looked left and right, searching for an opening or a path. Finally, after several minutes she found a clearing on her side of the road. She drove her truck into the leaf- and branch-strewn path. The path narrowed as she continued about fifty feet until she could go no farther. Still, she thought it was perfect. She got out to further survey the spot. Alexa then walked back to the road, noticing that it could be easily navigated on foot. From the road she checked to see if her bright-red truck was visible. It was not.

She went back to her vehicle, backed it up, and drove eastbound. Nobody noticed her pull onto or off the road. At the Route 115 junction, she turned north toward home. As she continued on her way, she could see she was entering a more populated area with some residences. The homes were far apart from each other, all a blend of sizes and styles. She studied each one closely, until one caught her attention. At the end of a long driveway, she spotted a gray farm-style house with an adjacent barn. The home could not be seen by any neighbors, she noted. Behind the residence was a wooded forest hugging a still white-capped mountain.

The mailbox at the end of their driveway had the name *Barretts* on the side. Alexa drove down the driveway, parking in front of the house. The residence had an elliptical driveway in front, allowing for an easy turnaround without backing up. In front of the barn, she noticed an old, black, rusted pickup truck. She walked up the front steps onto an open deck. She knocked on the door and waited. After waiting a minute, she knocked again, harder.

Finally, an elderly man came to the door. He wore faded blue jeans and a flannel shirt.

"May I help you, young lady?"

"Yes, sir, are you Mr. Barrett?"

"Yes, I am. Do I know you?" he asked, puzzled. He did not get visitors.

"My name is Amanda. I was wondering if I could rent your barn," she asked politely.

"Rent the barn? What for?"

"I need a secure place to store my pickup truck for a couple of months. I would pay you good money."

"Barbara!" he called out as she waited on the porch.

A moment later Barbara Barrett appeared at her husband's side.

"Barb, she is offering to pay to use the barn."

"Come inside, dear," she said, visibly scolding her husband for being a poor host.

"Thank you, ma'am," Alexa said, stepping into the residence.

Alexa looked around, evaluating the site. There were several rooms and a staircase leading upstairs, no doubt to their bedroom, she thought. There was little natural light in the residence. One lamp illuminated the hallway. The house had a creaky wooden floor that sagged as they walked on it.

They ushered her into their living room. Mrs. Barrett took a stack of newspapers off the couch to make room for Alexa. As she sat down, she noted that housekeeping was not Mrs. Barrett's strong suit.

"Now, what is this about?" Mrs. Barrett asked. It was clear she was in charge of the house.

"I work at the Bureau of Prisons, as you can see," she said, pointing to her uniform.

"Yes, I'm not that old," she cracked.

"I need a place to store my pickup truck. I'm getting a new car, and I need a safe place to store the truck until I decide what to do with it. I'm only allowed one parking spot at my apartment complex."

"I see."

Mr. Barrett sat quietly while his wife conducted her interrogation.

"How long and how much?" she asked directly.

"I can give you two hundred right now. Just for two months." As she spoke, Alexa pulled out two fresh one hundred-dollar bills. She could see their eyes widen.

"She can keep it here longer, don't you think, Barb," he suggested.

"I think we can do that," Mrs. Barrett stated, reaching over as Alexa handed her the cash.

"Do you two live alone?" she inquired.

"Yes. We have a daughter, but she lives in Denver."

Alexa was pleased with their answer. She rose to leave.

"Thank you so much."

"When can we expect the truck? So I can clean out the barn," Mr. Barrett offered.

"I'll be back in three days."

They escorted her to their front door. She shook their hands and walked back to her truck. As she drove off, the Barretts were ecstatic at their sudden luck. They hadn't used the barn for any real purpose in years. They spent the rest of the day marveling at their good fortune.

—

After her abrupt and unceremonious dismissal from the NSA, Suzanne Goldwein had another plan. The information she needed, she came to realize, was just as available through traditional cyber sleuthing. There was no need to access the NSA's secret database. Given that she now knew which computers had been used by their hunted coyote, it was a simple matter. All she need do was access those computers and download the information. Absent that possibility, she could just review the browsing history of the four computers at the Reston Library. Even when the browser's history is wiped clean, it can be restored. The information remains in play until it is overwritten.

When she arrived at the library, Geller went back to the Internet stations. She checked out the four computers, and they were all available. Just as when she was last at the scene of the crime, she thought to herself. She discreetly pulled out her specially enhanced *Ironkey* flash drive and inserted it into the first computer. The *Ironkey's* encryption is so secure it would take the NSA weeks to decipher, *if* they could first crack her password. A special program ensured that after ten unsuccessful password attempts, all the data on it is wiped clean. Further, the *Ironkey* would immediately notify her of any malware on the computers she was hacking. This assured her that if the Bureau had anticipated her actions and then placed a virus on the computers, she would know.

Her flash drive's program started aggressively searching and then downloading all of the data on the computer. She repeated the procedure for each computer.

Once finished, she went back to her hotel room and started a review of the files on her laptop. She spent the entire day this way, taking notes and attempting to discern what was related to their fugitive and what was innocent. Perhaps, she hoped, something would surface that could be useful.

———

That evening, Michael Wallace rolled back and forth in his bunk fitfully. He was convinced that Sullivan was trying to manipulate him, but his isolation had clouded his judgment. What was the agent's final agenda? He leaned toward the theory that he was still hunting his sister. But what if she had been captured as they had said? He could not be certain. He knew Alexa was resourceful, but she was alone. Perhaps he had squandered his only opportunity to communicate with her. His pride had possibly closed the door on the chance. He agonized over his decision to sabotage the letter. He looked up at the ceiling, a tear forming in the corner of his eye.

———

Alexa browsed through the men's shoe section of *Gordmans* department store in Colorado Springs with a sense of purpose. She knew that if her plan was successful, her brother would need a change of clothes. In her shopping cart, Alexa had already deposited two pairs of blue jeans, five collared shirts of different colors, a package of men's underwear, a dozen white socks, five plain white T-shirts, and a men's reversible black-and-brown belt.

After inspecting several pairs of shoes, she selected a gray-and-silver pair of sneakers, size ten.

In the sporting goods section, Alexa selected a two-man camping tent, a pair of sleeping bags, water proof matches, a lantern, and other camping gear.

As Alexa made her way toward the checkout registers, her phone started vibrating. She looked at the screen and saw that it was David. She picked up on the second ring.

"Hi, Dave!"

"Hey there," he said quietly.

"I haven't heard from you in a couple of days," she said.

"I was about to say the same thing."

"I've been so busy with my new job, sweetie."

"I understand." He smiled.

"I've missed you," she said. "We should meet tomorrow night."

Sutter perked up. He had been worried when he hadn't heard from her.

"Sure," he answered eagerly.

"Listen, I have to ask you for a favor."

"Of course, what is it, Amanda?"

"It's a big favor, sweetie."

"What is it?"

"I need to borrow your car."

"How come?"

"I need to drop my truck off tomorrow. It needs some work, and it has to be left overnight. Maybe two nights."

"Let me think." He paused.

"What about your parents? Maybe they could loan you their car."

"I will have to ask them."

"I would make it up to you."

Dave thought about the situation for a moment, finally coming up with an idea.

"I could meet you at your place tomorrow night. You could take my car to work. Then in the morning, I could ask my parents to pick me up."

Alexa smiled at his cleverness.

"I see what you're doing, Dave." She chuckled playfully.

"Just thinking."

"Sure you are."

"Well?"

"That's a good idea, Dave. It's a date."

As she hung up with Dave, she realized everything was falling into place. One more problem solved, she thought.

THIRTY THREE

Forty-Eight Hours

The next morning, Alexa pulled her red pickup truck into the Supermax employees' parking lot as she always had. This time, however, the bed of the truck contained one backpack with her personal belongings and another for her brother. In addition she had two large bags packed with the medical and camping equipment she had purchased. She had drawn her tarp over the truck bed to conceal her payload. Under her seat she had another bag with her weapons and a change of clothes.

She got out of the truck and quickly distanced herself from it, hoping nobody would tie her to it. To her relief, nobody had yet asked her about the change in her truck's color.

Once inside the facility, she was introduced to her new supervisor, Sergeant Barringer. He introduced her to the kitchen staff from whom she would be retrieving the inmate's meals. He toured her through tiers one and two, showing her how to open the aperture in the cell doors.

He stopped in front of an empty cell for demonstration purposes.

"Each cart will have twenty trays. You will slip the tray through this opening," he said, pulling a lever to the left.

She nodded.

"You will not have any verbal interaction with inmates."

"Understood."

"They will try and engage with you, Fisher." He looked directly at her.

"Yes, sir."

"OK then," he said.

"I'm ready, sir," she replied eagerly.

"Very well. You will conduct the next meal delivery, in two hours."

———

Sullivan and Riley met in the hotel lounge at nine o'clock, as prearranged. They feasted at the complimentary breakfast buffet, eating scrambled eggs, bacon, and toast. They talked about how to pass the day since they had decided to wait another twenty-four hours before approaching Wallace again. They wanted Wallace to believe it was possible his letter was delivered. Riley was perusing a tourist brochure, trying to pick a spot to visit, when Sullivan's phone started vibrating on the table.

Sullivan picked up the phone. He could see it was Goldwein calling.

"Suzanne," he said. "Good to hear from you."

"You too." She chuckled. "How's Colorado?"

"Too soon to say."

"Well, I've got some leads for you, if you have the time."

"Seriously?"

"Yes."

"I'm listening."

Riley's attention was now entirely focused on Sullivan's conversation.

"Do you have a pen and paper?"

Sullivan took some notes, hung up the phone, and looked at Riley.

"Well?" Riley asked.

"We won't be touring today." Sullivan rubbed his hands together and got out of his chair.

———

Michael Wallace's torment had prevented him from sleeping well. He was in a state of depression. He lay in his bunk in despair. Even his mental architectural tricks had eluded him. He had no energy for them. He heard the clanging sound of the food tray that brought his meal. He could hear the food tray pass into his cell. Yet he remained immobile. He had no energy or appetite. The food stayed where it was for two hours before he rolled out of his bunk and shuffled to the tray. Something immediately caught his attention. On the tray, next to his plate, was a small rolled-up piece of paper. He walked to his bunk with his tray and sat down. Slowly, he opened up the paper and read the message: *"Twenty-four hours. Be ready. Alexa."*

His jaw dropped. Wallace looked toward the door, but there was nobody there. He looked at his watch. It was two o'clock. Damn, he thought, the message had sat there for two hours. His mind raced. Could it be a trick? He looked at the note again and realized it was his sister's handwriting. She had come through for him.

He was still in a heightened state of excitement as he took the note and ate it.

———

Riley sat in the passenger seat in the visitors' parking lot of the *Fountainhead* apartment complex, listening as Sullivan related what Goldwein had told him. He nodded as he heard the details.

"So this is one of three Colorado apartment complexes researched from one of those computers?"

"That's right."

"It sounds slim."

"Well, it's something."

"What's Goldwein's theory?"

"She says that there were multiple searches for things in Colorado. She thinks our fugitive may have moved here, or is planning to."

"A lot of people visit that library."

"Yes, but it stands to reason that she would want to be near her brother."

"Why this place first?"

"No reason." Sullivan shrugged. "I just picked randomly."

"You realize we have no credentials or authority, right?"

"We'll improvise."

"OK then."

They got out of their car and went into the *Fountainhead* complex. Following a sign, they walked through a glass door and into the *Fountainhead* administration offices. Behind the counter sat a female in her sixties. A pair of reading glasses dangled from a silver chain around her neck, swaying gently. She turned her attention to her visitors as they stood by the counter.

"May I help you?" she asked helpfully.

She rose from her chair and walked over to the counter.

"I hope so," Sullivan said.

"Are you looking for an apartment?"

"Not exactly. My name is Carlos Sullivan. I'm trying to find a young lady who may have moved here recently."

Her shoulders slumped slightly. She shook her head.

"We really can't give any information out on our residents."

"I'm trying to help this young lady out," Sullivan continued. "You see, I hit her car a few days ago, and I lost her contact information. For insurance purposes I'm trying to get in touch with her."

"Do you have her name?"

"I'm afraid I forgot it."

Riley watched silently as Sullivan struggled with the situation.

"I'm sorry, sir."

"Well, can you tell me if any female in her twenties moved here in the last thirty days?" Sullivan's eyes widened, pleading with her.

"No, I can't tell you that, sir."

"Would you be in a position to know that?" Sullivan persisted.

"Yes, but I can't discuss our tenants." Her position was hardening.

"Well, thank you anyway," Sullivan said.

They walked out of the office into the hallway.

"What do you think?" Sullivan asked.

"Me? You're the lie-detector guy—what do you think?"

"I think all she had to say was that nobody like that has moved in here recently." He smiled.

"And she didn't." Riley nodded his head.

"If she had said that, she could have gotten rid of us and not violated any tenant's privacy."

"So we are on to something"

"I would say so, Riley."

———

At exactly three o'clock, Alexa walked out of the Supermax facility, her shift having ended. Typically, she made it a habit of hanging around for a few minutes after her shift in an attempt to make a good impression. However, now that her mission had turned operational, her focus intensified. She had no time for trivialities.

Driving east on Route 50 and using her trip odometer, she quickly found the spot she had staked out earlier. She pulled over onto the breakdown lane to wait for a car behind her to pass by. Once the road was clear, she drove into the concealed spot and parked her vehicle. She reached for the bag under her seat and quickly changed into civilian clothes. The uniform, she put in the bag. She also took her stun gun and stash of fentanyl and put that in the same bag. She then walked through the woods until she found a hollowed-out log. She pulled it to the road, blocking the entrance to the path.

She grabbed the bag with her uniform and started walking east. She knew this was one part of her plan that relied on luck rather than precision. She could not ask Dave to pick her up there. He would ask too many questions. She decided she would simply walk with the hope that a Good Samaritan would eventually offer her a ride. After walking for five miles, she was starting to think she would be on foot all night. Eventually, however, a silver Cadillac sedan pulled up next to her.

She looked over at the man driving, who rolled the passenger window down. He was in his late sixties and sported a polo shirt and blue jeans. He wore large black-rimmed glasses. His hair was gray and neatly trimmed. She quickly profiled him as more avuncular than creepy.

"Young lady," he called out, "do you need a ride?"

"That's so kind. My car broke down."

"Where are you headed?"

"Colorado Springs."

"Oh my, that's quite a way." He grimaced.

"Can you take me partway?"

He paused for a moment, thinking. "Young lady, I have a daughter myself. I will take you the whole way."

"That's wonderful! I can give you gas money." She gushed.

"No need, miss. This will be my good deed for the day."

She jumped in the passenger seat.

"My name is George."

"I'm Amanda," she said, placing her bag on the floor.

With that, they headed toward Colorado Springs.

———

After driving together from Boston to Colorado, Sullivan and Riley had each exhausted their collection of personal war stories. So as they sat in their car for hours outside the *Fountainhead* complex, they did so silently. Riley browsed the Internet through his smartphone. Sullivan played with the radio, scanning each car as it entered the parking lot. Riley's assignment was to watch the people leaving the building. After several hours they had no luck.

As the hour approached five, they perked up slightly. Perhaps their fugitive had a job. If so it was likely she would be getting out of work soon. They each had the same thought as they watched the radio clock advance.

———

George and Alexa made small talk as he drove them north into Colorado Springs. Alexa learned that George had a daughter who was only a few years older than she was. She was a nurse in Des Moines. He and his wife were lifelong Colorado residents. She listened attentively, grateful that she had found her Good Samaritan. She was looking forward to a relaxing bath before Dave arrived for dinner.

Finally, she thought, as they approached the large sign: "*Fountainhead Deluxe Apartments.*"

"That's it, there on the right," she said, pointing.

George took a right turn into the parking complex. Immediately, Alexa saw them, parked about three hundred feet away. Her sharp eyes instantly recognized the green Chevy Impala with Massachusetts license plates. She reflexively hunched down in her seat.

"What's wrong?" George asked, concerned.

"Keep driving, George!" she yelled.

"Why?"

"I have an ex-boyfriend who's been stalking me," she cried.

"Oh my, what do I do?"

"Just drive us out of here."

As they passed his car, Sullivan could see an older gentleman driving alone. He noticed, however, that he seemed to be talking to himself. He poked Riley with his elbow.

George drove around the lot and then headed back the way they came in.

"Did you notice that, Riley?"

"He's probably just lost."

"Let's check it out anyway." Sullivan pulled out and gunned the engine.

In less than a minute, they were on the Cadillac's tail as it approached an intersection. George stopped as he heard the sound of screeching tires. Sullivan drove around the Cadillac's right and blocked him from moving. Guns drawn, Sullivan and Riley approached the car. Riley put his gun to George's window while Sullivan looked in the car. It was empty.

"False alarm!" Sullivan yelled, banging the top of the Cadillac with his free hand.

"Sorry, sir," Riley said to George.

They got in their Impala and drove back to the *Fountainhead*, hoping that nobody had called the police.

George was shaken to the core. He started panting until finally composing himself. He pulled his car back onto the freeway headed south and home with quite a story to tell his wife. From a nearby set of bushes, Alexa had watched the action unfold. Once George had pulled out of the complex, she pushed the door open and jumped out of the car. She rolled into the brush before they could see her.

She reached for her phone and called her one reliable contact. He answered on the first ring.

"Dave," she said, "change of plans."

THIRTY FOUR

Refuge

As David worked in the kitchen, preparing her another one of his special meals, Alexa sat in his living room, lost in thought. She quickly surmised that her pursuers had managed to use the Internet to track her. There was no other explanation. She kicked herself for foolishly thinking she could avoid detection by using public networks. Still, they must not know about her employment. If that were the case, the game would be over. She knew it was only a matter of time, however. As she pondered the situation, she unconsciously put her hand to her throat as if a noose were around her neck.

Her only hope was to accomplish her mission before her enemies connected all the dots. That was outside her sphere of control as her father used to say. She would stay focused on her remaining tasks.

One thing she did know for certain. Without David she could not have come this far. Now, his apartment served as her refuge. She could never go back to the *Fountainhead*. As she considered this, she heard him calling to her.

"So what exactly is wrong with your truck?"

"Sweetie, I don't know about cars. I was told it's something about the transmission."

"Well, don't worry, my parents are loaning me one of their cars for a couple of days."

"That's so nice of them. I can't wait to meet them." She knew full well that would never happen.

"So you are going to drive all the way to Florence from here tomorrow?"

"No choice."

"Why don't you take a day off. We can just relax."

"I can't, Dave. I'm too new."

"I understand."

Leaving the kitchen for a moment, Sutter came over to her and sat down next to Alexa, putting an arm around her.

"I'm glad that you feel you can count on me."

"Dave, you have no idea."

He kissed her on the forehead before getting up again to check on the meal he was preparing. With every dinner he prepared for her, he poured out his heart. His wish was that the food would serve as an aphrodisiac. He hoped it was only a matter of time.

Alexa could hear the steak he was cooking sizzling on the stove. A slight aroma of garlic permeated the room from the mashed potatoes he was preparing as a side dish.

As she went over her remaining tasks in her head, she realized she was getting hungry. Her father had always taught his children to eat well before any operation. He always said that once a mission is operational, you never know when you will have a chance to refuel. She thought of this as she leaned back on the couch, waiting for what she was becoming accustomed to—another one of Dave's mouth-watering feasts.

Sullivan and Riley sat at a booth at *Anthony's Pizzeria*, waiting patiently for the pepperoni-and-mushroom pizza they had ordered. *Anthony's* was less than a mile from the *Fountainhead* apartment complex. They shared a pitcher of Miller Lite, Sullivan pouring the glasses. In addition to the beer, they shared the disappointment of a long and frustrating surveillance.

"So what now?" Riley asked, sipping his beer.

"We keep sitting on the apartment complex."

"What about going to see Wallace tomorrow?"

"That can wait a day. Let him stew a little more."

Riley shrugged approval.

"Sounds good."

"Let's give this *Fountainhead* place one more day. Maybe we will get lucky."

"Sure, Sully."

The pizza's arrival caused them both to smile. It came piping hot with a side of cheese bread. They had the same thought. The day was ending on a good note.

———

Michael Wallace could barely contain himself. He lay on his bunk, looking up to the stars in the clear night sky. He smiled at the thought that his instincts, despite the prolonged isolation, were still intact. Sullivan *had* been messing with him. The thought occurred to him that perhaps one day soon he would have an opportunity to come through on his threat. He decided that his beef with Agent Sullivan was personal after all.

He spent the next several hours wondering what his sister had in store for him. He finally closed his eyes and rested peacefully.

THIRTY FIVE

Twenty-Four Hours

Alexa was energized as she arrived to work in Sutter's loaner, a gray Honda Civic sedan. It drove well, she thought. More importantly, nobody noticed her as she parked and went into the facility. The last thing she needed was questions about her truck.

This would be her second and last day working the food service. According to the schedule, tomorrow she would be working the sally port and perimeter. She crossed her fingers that the schedule would not be changed as her mission depended on it.

When the lunch service was ready, Alexa was again summoned to deliver the food trays. She pushed the cart down the corridor, dutifully placing a tray in each cell. Per instructions she said nothing, even when some of the inmates called to her. It was as if they could smell a female through the steel door, she thought to herself.

Michael could hear the tray approaching outside in the corridor. It had a slight squeak in one of the wheels. He looked at his watch. It was exactly twenty-four hours since he received the note. It must be Alexa, he hoped.

As Alexa opened the small aperture and slid the tray into the cell, Michael remained in his bunk. He did not want to jeopardize the mission by being overly eager. Perhaps she was accompanied on her rounds, and another guard might notice something. So he waited.

Once he heard the cart wheeled away from his cell, he finally went and retrieved his food. He sat with the tray in his lap. Again he saw a rolled-up note. Next to it was a small pill.

He unrolled the paper and read the secret missive: *"Take this pill at exactly 12:25 p.m. tomorrow. Alexa."*

His eyes widened as he smiled. As before, he quickly swallowed the note.

———

Detective Juan Dominguez sat at his small metal desk inside the Boston Police area A-1 station house, a block from City Hall Plaza. He had stacks of reports to complete and little time for them. His biggest concern of late was the rising use of contaminated heroin. A string of recent overdose deaths had left pockets of the city reeling. Although drug investigations were not complicated, they were time intensive. They required the use of informants or undercover officers to make covert drug purchases. Each of those encounters carried inherent dangers. Further, prosecutors now demanded that such transactions be recorded, with video preferably. Each of those tapes needed to be logged and cataloged accurately. He looked at his stack of files and then at his watch, wondering if he would ever get home.

As he prepared to put his files away for the night, he felt the phone on his desk vibrating. It was an unknown number to him, although the area code indicated the call was from the city.

Tired, he reluctantly picked up the phone.

"This is Dominguez."

He strained to hear the soft voice on the other end of the line.

"It's Jody Turner," she whispered.

"Ms. Turner." He perked up. "I'm glad you called."

"I know where they are."

The detective pulled out his small notebook. Home could wait.

———

After another fruitless day at the *Fountainhead* complex; both Sullivan and Riley were ready to quit for the day. They seemed no closer to catching their elusive coyote. Sullivan had started to doubt the entire Colorado expedition. At least he knew that he had gotten under Wallace's skin. That was their consolation. As the sun set on the *Fountainhead* parking lot, they decided to throw in the towel.

"Dinner?" Sullivan asked.

"Drinks?"

"On me, buddy."

"Sounds like a plan."

They pulled out of the parking lot, hungry and thirsty, bound for their hotel.

———

Trish O'Keefe and Jimmy Conrad sat in a dark corner booth of the *Kelly Tavern*, holding hands. The FBI suspensions had shaken O'Keefe more than Conrad, despite the fact that she had been the one spared.

The dinner crowd at the bar was focused on the Bruins play-off game. The patrons were electrified. The series was tied at three games each. The Bruins, playing at home, desperately needed a win to advance to the next round. Conrad and O'Keefe had other concerns. They blocked out the cheering and hollering without effort, as they waited for their meals.

"Everything is going to work out, Trish."

"You think?"

"The fact is, we came close to getting her. The director will take that into consideration."

"True."

"We just need something to break our way, and we will catch her."

Conrad had a determined look on his face.

"I hope so because this is killing me."

Just as she said this, Conrad's phone started vibrating on the table. Normally, he did not take calls when he was on a date with Trish, but the circumstances demanded it now. He could see from the caller ID that it was Detective Dominguez. He answered immediately.

"Conrad here."

O'Keefe could see Conrad's eyes widen as he listened to the detective. He kept nodding his head as he strained to hear over the ambient noise in the restaurant. After a minute, he put the phone down.

"Well?"

"That was Dominguez," he said calmly.

"Good news?" she said excitedly.

"He found them."

"So what are you doing here?" she chided.

"Take it home for me, baby," he said.

"Go, Jimmy. You have work to do." She waved to the door.

With that, Conrad got up and walked with a renewed purpose to the exit.

THIRTY SIX

Sixteen Hours and the Prisoner's Dilemma

Alexa sat in the driver's seat of the loaned Honda, with the seat leaned back. She watched the few cars that passed by with suspicion, taking note of their make and model. She saw no police cruisers, which was a good sign given that she was only three blocks from the Florence Police Department.

She saw a light on in the window of her target residence, a second-floor rental unit. She checked her watch, which blinked eight thirty. In less than sixteen hours, her escape plan would be launched. She tried keeping her excitement in check. She knew that anything could still go wrong.

Wearing dark blue jeans and a black hoodie, which she pulled over her head, she got out of the car and walked into the small apartment building. There were two units on the first floor and a common stairwell leading to two additional units on the second floor. She quickly walked up the carpeted stairs, and found unit 2B. She rapped on the door and waited.

Doctor Winchester opened the door and looked down at his visitor with a bewildered look. She seemed vaguely familiar.

"Can I help you?"

"Yes, actually," she answered. With one quick motion, she lunged at him with her stun gun.

The shock jolted him back and onto the floor. She walked inside and closed the door to the apartment. After determining that he was in fact alone, as she had expected, she reached down and pulled the belt off his pants. He was stunned but conscious. She knelt behind him and wrapped the belt around his neck.

He could not believe what was happening to him. He reached for the belt, but she kept cinching it tighter, squeezing the life out of him. He was too weak to resist and started to lose consciousness. He tried speaking but could not. With his last ounce of strength, he started kicking, but she was behind him. It had no effect. Lastly, he twitched uncontrollably, like a fish on the deck of a boat.

When his body finally fell limp, Alexa checked his pulse and confirmed that he had expired. She looked down at him with contempt.

"You can help me by dying," she whispered.

—

When an interrogator is presented with two captured suspects linked to the same crime, this scenario is known as *the prisoner's dilemma*. Each suspect is kept in a separate holding room. The dilemma is the same for each suspect. Do I keep quiet, hoping that my partner will also keep quiet? Or do I talk and get the better deal? Each knows that their confederate is making the same calculation. Only in rare cases does a suspect have complete confidence that his partner will not crack. This dynamic is exploited routinely by investigators seeking to break a suspect.

Detective Dominguez and Jimmy Conrad were well versed in the use of this technique as they had used it together in the past. Conrad now sat across from Sonny Turner while Dominguez worked the room with Tammy Smith.

Conrad looked sternly at Sonny as he sat with his head down. He had been partying all day and was still somewhat buzzed. Normally, an interrogation would occur once the suspect is sober. But Conrad knew there was no time to waste. They had been itching for this moment for quite a while.

"Sonny."

"What?"

"You want to make a deal, right?"

"Whatever, man, you got me." Sonny seemed resigned.

"No, Sonny, this isn't about the heroin they found on you."

"It's not?" He lifted his head and squinted at Conrad.

"No, it's not." He said with a serious tone.

"What's it about?" Sonny perked up slightly, worried that he was in deeper trouble than he initially thought.

"This is about the agent that was killed."

"That female? I don't know anything about it." He fidgeted nervously.

"Really? Because Tammy is being a little more cooperative."

Conrad pointed to the door.

"My partner is talking to her right now."

———

Tammy Smith sat with arms crossed, her face looking down, defiantly. Dominguez sat across from her, his legs crossed comfortably, a note pad in his hand.

"Tammy, there is no reason you have to take the rap for murder."

She looked up, confused.

"Murder! What are you talking about?"

"The agent that was killed." He looked at her calmly.

"What does that have to do with me?" she yelled.

"If you had something to do with her being killed, it was probably Sonny's idea."

"We had nothing to do with that!"

A vein in her neck started visibly pulsating.

"So you were just a witness?" he offered.

"Yes!" she blurted out. "Just witnesses."

"So what did you see?"

"Nothing."

"Tammy, you just said you were a witness." He leaned in.

"No, no…" she stammered, "you're confusing me!"

Tammy slammed her hand against the table. Her face turned bright red, and she started breathing heavily. She was having a tantrum, and Dominguez decided to turn up the pressure. He started texting.

"What are you doing?" she yelled.

"Nothing, don't worry," he answered calmly.

"What are you texting!"

———

Conrad's phone chirped and flashed the text seconds later. He grinned at the message: "*She said they were just witnesses.*"

Sonny sat in his chair, watching with growing concern as Conrad inspected his phone. His eyes could not have been wider if he had used hairpins to hold his eyelids open. A bead of sweat was forming on his forehead. He started feeling sick again as Conrad put the phone down.

"Tammy says you were just witnesses." Conrad said with a matter-of-fact tone.

"Fucking bitch!" he yelled across the room.

"It seems she's giving some sort of statement."

"All right, I'll tell you," he said, defeated.

"Tell me what, Sonny? We may not need your statement anymore."

"We *were* just witnesses," he said wearily.

Conrad took a moment to send Dominguez a return text: "*He cracked—come over.*"

"Tell me what happened, Sonny."

As Sonny took a moment to compose himself, Dominguez walked into the room.

"He's going to talk, *right*, Sonny." Conrad glared over at him.

Dominguez glared even harder and pointed his finger at Sonny.

"It better be the same story Tammy just told me."

"OK, man."

"Let's hear it."

"We were coming out of my mom's apartment," he started, "and we looked across the street. That female agent lives across from us."

"How did you know she's an FBI agent?" Conrad asked.

"Are you kidding? Everyone knew she was a fed."

"Go on," Dominguez ordered.

"There was a female, not the agent. She was jumping up to the small window ledge. She could really leap, man."

Conrad and Dominguez looked at each other, signaling for him to continue.

"The ledge is narrow, so she kept falling off. So this is crazy, but you gotta believe me. She calls us over."

"You talked to her?" Dominguez asked.

"Yeah, she said she was the agent's sister. Said she wanted to surprise her and couldn't find the key."

"So you helped her?" Conrad was furious.

"We never thought anything of it. She seemed normal!" he pleaded.

"So what happened?"

"We helped her up to the ledge so she could slide the window open."

Conrad's face was bright red. His eyes seemed about to explode. He stood over Sonny, Dominguez next to him.

"Why would you do that?" he yelled.

Sonny felt that Conrad was about to reach over and pummel him. He stretched his arms out, palms up, pleading.

"She showed us a badge! She was a cop!"

Upon hearing this, Conrad and Dominguez, stunned, slowly sat down.

———

Trish O'Keefe was getting ready for bed when her house phone rang loudly. She reached over, concerned. Perhaps something happened to Jimmy, she worried, as she saw his number flash on the phone's display.

She answered immediately.

"Jimmy, is everything all right?"

"Yeah, Trish, but I'm going to need your help."

THIRTY SEVEN

Countdown

The morning sun shone brightly on the hills of Fremont County, Colorado. Alexa had been driving with the window down, enjoying a blast of fresh air. Her thoughts were on how Dave woke her with a gentle kiss on the forehead. Then, before leaving, he kissed her again at the door. Unbeknown to him, it would be their last embrace.

After pulling into the prison's parking lot for the last time, Alexa took the key to the Honda and left it in the glove box. She hoped that after she was long gone, the authorities would eventually return the car to David. She knew he would be put under intense scrutiny, suspected of having helped her. It was the least she could do, she thought. She thought back to the dream she had days earlier and realized its meaning. She would not hurt him.

David had taken a picture of them together at a local park, which Alexa kept in her wallet. Now, as she was prepared to embark on a new chapter in her life, she looked at the picture one last time. She took the picture and placed it underneath the key. There was no turning back.

Alexa walked into the ADX Supermax one final time.

A wave of ominous dark clouds had descended on the city of Boston that morning. Light raindrops started to pelt the streets, causing small puddles to form in the city's ubiquitous potholes. After suffering from the most brutal winter in the history of the city, potholes had become winter's last unwanted gift. The plowing, salting, and sanding had left the city with street craters of all sizes and shapes.

Conrad and Dominguez, having slept in the station house, looked out the window, grateful that they were indoors. Conrad eagerly watched for any sign of O'Keefe.

Conrad drank orange juice. Dominguez held his Dunkin' Donuts coffee cup like a prize. He looked over at Conrad.

"Is she coming?"

"She will be here."

"It's just as well those two got their rest. Perhaps their memories will be sharper."

It was almost ten o'clock when O'Keefe finally walked into the station house. She had the weary look of someone who had slept little that night.

"I was getting worried," Conrad said.

O'Keefe looked at them both like a scolding mother.

"Are you guys aware of how many badges there are in this country?"

"Not really," Dominguez chimed in.

"Well, there are thousands."

"Thousands?" Conrad said sheepishly.

"Yes, if you include local police departments, municipal police, transit police, county sheriffs' departments, state police, federal, tribal—"

"We get it, Trish." Conrad cut her off.

Trish reached into her purse and pulled out a green thumb drive.

"Well, they are all in here." She smiled.

"Great," Dominguez offered.

"Let's start with Virginia and Colorado Police."

"Good thinking, Trish." Conrad beamed.

They escorted her toward the interview room where Sonny and Tammy were waiting.

Once Sullivan heard Conrad's latest intriguing news, he and Riley decided it would be prudent to hold off any further surveillances or interviews. Perhaps Conrad's lead would offer them a new avenue of investigation. Or a new angle to continue their interviews with Michael Wallace. Much depended, of course, on the continued cooperation of their new witnesses. With this in mind, they decided to have brunch at a diner in Florence, close to the prison.

In criminal law a person's intent is critical in any decision to prosecute an offender. The Latin phrase *mens rea* means "*guilty mind*" and is the deciding factor in whether charges are filed against a person and, if so, to what degree. After hearing Detective Dominguez's briefing, Assistant District Attorney (ADA) Gregory Vien decided that if Sonny was being truthful, there was no intent on their part to harm Agent Fuller. To the extent that they were duped by Alexa Wallace, they were themselves victims. They had become unwitting coconspirators. In order to cement their cooperation, he had agreed to extend Sonny and Tammy immunity in the Fuller matter. Further, he also agreed to probation for the heroin-possession charges.

Despite her initial hostility, Tammy Smith agreed to join Team Conrad-Dominguez once she was informed of the deal. Sonny and Tammy sat side by side across from ADA Vien, Detective Dominguez, Conrad, and O'Keefe. They were feeling better after a good night's sleep in their separate cells.

"Sonny," Dominguez started, "this is the prosecutor I told you about, ADA Vien."

"OK," Sonny said.

Tammy nodded silently.

"Mr. Turner, if you cooperate completely with these officers, you will get the deal you were promised."

"Yeah, we have to pick out the badge, like they said."

MICHAEL C. DE LA PENA

"What if we can't pick it out?" Tammy expressed her latent skepticism.

"So long as you honestly try," Vien stressed.

"We'll try."

"Do you understand this is very important?" Conrad added.

"About that…" Sonny fidgeted. "Isn't there a reward for this woman?"

Conrad looked at Dominguez and then over to O'Keefe. It was clear to them that Sonny's thinking had cleared up considerably.

"If your information leads to her arrest, then, yes, there is a reward."

"How much?" Tammy asked, now clearly engaged.

"Ten million dollars." Conrad gulped, horrified at the prospect of two junkies getting that kind of money.

Tammy eagerly smacked her hands together.

"Damn!" she shouted. "What are we waiting for?"

———

Michael Wallace checked his watch one more time. In less than an hour, he was to take the pill Alexa had secretly given him. He inspected it closely one more time. He could see that whatever was in the pill did not fill it completely. The weight had been altered. He estimated that it was at half strength. After thinking about the situation, he had come to realize that the pill was meant to sicken him. He also surmised that by taking the pill at 12:25 p.m., he would have already been given his lunch. Therefore, she wanted him to have some food in his stomach, perhaps to mitigate the ill effects. Further, since cell checks were conducted every thirty minutes, she intended for the guards to quickly notice his malady.

He had already decided to help the situation along by making a commotion once he got sick. He could not risk having the guard miss his illness. It was clear to him that her scheme involved having him transported to the infirmary. From there, she must have arranged a secondary plan.

He bit his nails, wondering if he would soon be a free man. He glanced once more at his timepiece. It was a quarter to twelve.

He prepared himself for the mission by initiating a mental countdown.

THIRTY EIGHT

Risk

Sergeant Alex Brissey inspected his new trainee as she stood before him, extending her hand. He had heard good things about her, but still he preferred to make his own judgments. The first thing he noticed was that her boots were polished to a bright sheen. This in itself impressed him. Most officers had long ago given up on these small details.

"Nice to meet you, Amanda," he said.

They shook hands, and he waved her over to the main sally port.

"Follow me."

He used his passkey to open the steel door leading into the central sally port. It was essentially a large garage bay into which transport vehicles were driven and secured. Once they were in the bay, an outer gate slid down, locking the vehicle in securely. The gate was only opened when visual confirmation was made that it was one of the prison's vehicles. The sergeant spent several minutes going over the protocols with Alexa.

He then walked her to a small adjacent room, again secured with a prison key. The sign above the door read *Weapons Room*. Only the sergeant on duty had a key to the room.

Once inside the room, the sergeant's tone became more serious.

"As you know, Amanda, BOP rules restrict weapons in all federal penitentiaries."

"Yes, sir. Weapons are only carried when transporting a prisoner into or out of the facility."

"That's right. Never, never, does a weapon go past that door."

He pointed at the entrance into the prison hallway for emphasis.

"Understood, sir."

As he walked her out of the room, she quickly glanced at her digital watch and smiled. It blinked twelve o'clock exactly.

———

Having been placed in separate rooms, each with a laptop, Tammy and Sonny began reviewing badges. O'Keefe had loaded each computer with the images of badges she amassed over the course of the prior evening. They had both agreed that the badge was yellowish in color, shaped more like a star than a shield. Sonny was also convinced there was an animal in the center of the badge. Other than that, they could offer no detail. The hope was that actually seeing the badge again would trigger a memory.

O'Keefe had arranged for Sonny to start viewing badges from the state of Virginia. Tammy was reviewing Colorado badges. After two hours neither could point to a particular shield.

Conrad sat next to O'Keefe as Sonny clicked the computer's mouse, each click flashing a different image. One badge at a time, Sonny scrutinized each picture. The idea of possibly cashing in on the reward money seemed to have energized him.

The wall clock on the far end of the interview room slowly advanced the time.

It was two o'clock Eastern Standard Time.

———

Two thousand miles away, the hands of Michael's watch crawled to the twelve o'clock position. As they did, he heard the sound he had been waiting for. The squeaky wheel of the metal food cart was making its appointed rounds. He sat patiently, and after a short wait, he heard his plastic food tray as it was placed in his cell.

He retrieved the tray and sat on his bunk. The meal consisted of an apple, a bowl of macaroni and cheese, a small piece of bread, and a plastic cup filled with water. He methodically began eating every last morsel of food, finishing in five minutes.

After swallowing the last of the food, he considered that in exactly twenty minutes, he would be taking a great leap of faith.

—

THIRTY NINE

Reward

Corrections Officer Walter Gibson was only twenty-three years old but already had two years on the job. His goal was to eventually become a Colorado state trooper like his father. With this in mind, he was fastidious in the performance of his duties. He knew his work record would be scrutinized down the line. On this day his duties included individual cell checks, which are required every thirty minutes without fail.

Given the impenetrable nature of the cells, the checks were primarily focused on ensuring the inmates did not commit suicide. Several years earlier, one of the inmates at the Supermax had bitten through his wrist and nicked his vein. The isolation had become too much for him, and he had gone mad. Fortunately, a cell check detected the attempt, and he was rushed to the infirmary in time. One of the senior officers had related the story to Gibson. The description of the inmate gnawing on his own flesh, pieces of skin scattered on the floor, with blood in his mouth and on his face like a vampire had left an impression.

As he approached tier two, cell ten, he heard a scream down the corridor. At first he couldn't believe what he was hearing. It was a loud yelp, like the sound of a dog whose tail had been stepped on. Then he heard a banging on cell-door thirteen.

Michael shrieked loudly and banged his food tray against the steel door. When Gibson looked in the cell, he was horrified.

Inmate Wallace was foaming at the mouth, and his skin was turning blue.

Gibson reached for his radio.

It was twelve thirty Mountain Standard Time.

———

Having started a review of federal law-enforcement badges, Sonny Turner had quickened the pace of his search. Instead of spending five seconds on each image, he was taking only two or three.

Conrad was reading a newspaper that he had placed flat on the table in front of him. He did this so he could still keep an eye on Sonny while he reviewed articles of interest. Despite Sonny's seeming eagerness to cooperate, Conrad knew he was still a junkie. Unreliable and unpredictable as Sonny was, Conrad had told Trish to go back to the office. He would call her if something developed. Reluctantly, she agreed.

As Conrad read an article about the Bruins victory in game seven of the play-off game the prior evening, he saw Sonny pause and move closer to the laptop screen. When Sonny looked over to him, he knew to get up.

He walked over and looked at the badge Sonny was pointing to.

The center of the badge had an eagle clutching an American flag. The top read, "*Department of Justice,*" and below it were the words, "*Federal Bureau of Prisons.*"

A sense of dread washed over him.

The clock on the lower right-hand side of the laptop flashed the time.

It was 2:35 p.m. Eastern Standard Time.

———

When Doctor Winchester failed to report to work that morning, the prison did not dispatch a SWAT team to find him. This was not the first time he had disappointed. Still, they had no reason to believe anything untoward had happened. Instead, the staff called his contact numbers. When he did not respond, they called Jo-Ann Salter to fill in.

Jo-Ann Salter had ten years' experience as a trauma nurse at the Florence Medical Center. With the birth of her third child, however, she decided that the daily grind was too much for her. Her superiors routinely asked her to work overtime, and the stress was wearing her thin. While the pay was rewarding, she needed to spend more time with her family. Consequently, she contracted with the ADX Supermax as an on-call nurse.

She had grown accustomed to working at the prison and knew that it was quite boring. Most of her work consisted of ensuring patients on medications received their proper doses.

Salter had expected her day to be quite routine—until the infirmary phone rang. This in itself was unusual. She looked at the phone on the wall, and the screen read, "*Command Center.*" She picked up on the third ring.

The voice on the other end of the phone was official sounding and serious.

"An inmate is in medical crisis. He's headed your way."

She hung up the phone and prepared a medical bed.

Having spent years in an emergency room, Salter had seen patients with all types and varieties of trauma. She was confident in her skills. Indeed, given what she had heard of Doctor Winchester, she believed the patient would be better off in her hands, regardless of his ailment. Nevertheless, she had also studied the prison medical protocols. A physician's presence gave the facility legal and political cover should a patient perish in their hands.

Salter had participated in several training scenarios that involved a medical crisis. In those scenarios, a licensed physician was always available. This was spelled out explicitly in the Federal Bureau of Prisons manual. It was the same manual that Alexa had studied thoroughly during her time at headquarters.

This requirement came to her mind as Officer Gibson and three other officers hurriedly carried Inmate Wallace into the infirmary on a stretcher.

The electric clock on the infirmary wall blinked the hour.

It was 12:36 p.m. Mountain Standard Time.

—

From her desk at the sally port, Alexa heard the commotion over her radio. She knew that her plan had been set in motion. More importantly, she heard the radio call to the adjacent administration building. She had no doubt that Warden Underwood was already on his way.

—

Having finished their late brunch, Sullivan and Riley paid their tab and tipped their waitress generously. They were enjoying fresh refills of coffee while they waited for word from Conrad. Riley was using his smartphone to review news from Boston. He was itching to get back home. His girlfriend had been nagging him about that to no end.

Sullivan was bored. He watched with curiosity as Riley scrolled through his phone.

"Riley, why did you decide to get into the tech program?"

"I've always been into gadgets, even as a kid," he said, looking up briefly. "Why did you get into the polygraph program?"

Sullivan thought for a moment. "I guess I like messing with a criminal's mind."

"Just criminals, of course." Riley joked.

Sullivan chuckled as Riley's phone started buzzing. It was his girlfriend, checking on him again.

While Riley chatted quietly, Sullivan turned his attention to the latest edition of the *Canon City Daily Record*, which he picked up at the diner's entrance. He browsed through local news stories. One article on page three, in particular, caught his attention.

Titled "*Unanswered Questions*," it detailed the stalled investigation into the death of Corrections Officer Wesley Hughes. Authorities had still not decided whether foul play was involved. The article detailed the cause of death, determined by the coroner to be an overdose of fentanyl. Given Hughes's exemplary work record; his previous drug test, which was negative; and the rarity of such deaths in Florence,

Colorado, the state police had taken over the investigation. Sullivan read the story with interest, when his phone vibrated on the counter in front of him. He could see it was Conrad.

"News?" Sullivan asked.

Riley's eyes widened as he saw Sullivan's reaction.

"Are you kidding, Jimmy?"

He quickly ended his conversation and put his phone down to listen, although he could only hear Sullivan's side of the conversation.

"Did the female confirm it?"

Sullivan shook his head and put the phone in his jacket pocket. He could see Riley was on the edge of his seat. Sullivan stood up and grabbed his car keys.

"Let's go."

"Where to?"

"The prison."

The old wooden clock behind the counter displayed the time.

It was 12:38 p.m. Mountain Standard Time.

———

When Warden Underwood arrived in the infirmary, he saw that two of his most senior lieutenants had beaten him to the scene. They flanked the infirmary bed on which Wallace was placed. Officer Gibson guarded the door as he walked in.

Underwood could clearly see that Inmate Wallace's pallor was ghoulishly white, his skin visibly clammy. Nurse Salter had already hooked him up to an IV line. She was taking his pulse as Underwood reached the bedside.

"How is he?"

Salter looked up at the warden with a worrisome look.

"He's weak, and his pulse is very low. His breathing is shallow."

"What happened?"

"I would say he's been poisoned, Warden."

"How in the hell?" He looked at his lieutenants, who shook their heads in disbelief.

"We could lose him," the nurse warned.

"Where on earth is the doctor?" Underwood looked about the room.

"He failed to report to work, sir," one of the lieutenants replied.

"I can't believe this shit!" He cursed, his hand on his forehead, thinking.

"Warden, medical protocols—"

"I know the fucking protocols." Underwood cut her off.

The warden looked at his officers, his brow furrowed. He looked at his watch. It read 12:42 p.m.

"Take him to a hospital," he ordered his officers. Then he pointed to the nurse. "You are going with him."

———

Sullivan's accelerator was touching the floor. He could go no faster. Fortunately, the road before them was not well traveled. Speeding at over one hundred miles per hour, Riley clutched the door handle tightly with his right hand. With his left, he dialed the warden's cell phone.

As cell phones are not allowed in the main facility, Underwood Warden felt it was wise to set a good example. He believed prison rules should be enforced uniformly through the ranks. Thusly, he had left his phone in his office when he got the emergency notification.

It rang gently in his top desk drawer until the call finally went to voice mail. When Riley heard the beep, he disconnected the call in disgust.

———

Sergeant Brissey sat at his desk, filling out a crossword puzzle. He was stuck on twenty-three across when his black desk phone rang, penetrating the silence. He reached over and answered instantly.

He listened carefully to the officer on the other end of the line.

Alexa watched keenly from across the room. Perhaps this was the call she was expecting, she thought hopefully. Her principal concern centered on whether she would be picked to ride in the van with her brother. She was new, after all, and this was an unusual situation. If she was not selected, she had already decided on a plan B. Her father had always taught her to have a secondary option. That plan involved leaving the facility, following the van, and then ramming it at some point along their route—a far riskier scenario much less likely to succeed. Nevertheless, this would be her only opportunity to get her brother outside the prison walls.

Brissey finally hung up the phone and looked over at Alexa. She could feel her breathing slow down as he looked at her.

"Fisher," he said, "we're going on a field trip."

Her heart skipped a beat as the sergeant rose from his chair. From where he was standing, he could not see the sparkle in Alexa's eyes.

———

In anticipation of Inmate Wallace's arrival, Sergeant Brissey checked out three forty-caliber Glock pistols from the weapons room. He holstered one, gave one to Alexa, and kept the third for another corrections officer who would be part of the transport team. Each prisoner transport required an escort of three armed officers.

As they stood next to each other, waiting and watching the entrance, Alexa worried for her brother. Had she given him too high a dose of fentanyl? She knew that despite her previous experiments, she was still guessing to some degree. Every person reacts differently to poison. She had to dose him with enough that he would require a doctor's attention. Yet if she gave him too much, it could be his demise. She crossed her fingers that the dose would be just enough to accomplish its purpose.

Just then, they heard the officers arriving on the other side of the door. Sergeant Brissey buzzed them in. They wheeled the collapsible stretcher into the sally port.

Immediately, she noticed her brother was in bad shape. The nurse had placed an oxygen mask over his face, but even through that she could see he was in distress. He was handcuffed to the metal bar on the side of the stretcher. She knew that was required during the transport.

Having already backed the transport van in and opened the rear doors, they quickly hustled Wallace inside, flattening the stretcher lower to the floor. Nurse Salter was at his side.

Sergeant Brissey picked Officer Gibson from among the escorting officers.

"Gibson"—he pointed—"you're coming with us."

Sergeant Brissey handed Gibson a weapon and holster. He then decided he would drive and got behind the wheel. After Gibson strapped the gun to his waist, he climbed into the van. Alexa followed him, pulling the van's rear doors closed. The white van had the words *Federal Bureau of Prisons* in black on both sides.

Once they were all in, the sergeant activated the sally port's garage doors. Alexa watched impatiently from the front passenger seat as the door slowly rose before them. The fifteen seconds this procedure took seemed like an eternity to her.

Finally, the door was fully opened and Sergeant Brissey drove out of the prison. Alexa took one last look at the facility as they pulled out. She looked at her watch. It was 12:50 p.m.

Michael Wallace was now outside the prison's walls.

FORTY

Freedom

Just as Michael Wallace's transport van departed, Sullivan was entering the prison on the exact opposite side of the facility. Sullivan's Impala screeched to a stop in front of the building's main entrance. The skid left tire marks on the pavement. Had he gotten any closer to the building, they would have parked in the reception area.

Sullivan and Riley ran inside. They recognized Officer Roach behind the desk from their previous visit. When he looked up from the computer screen, he could tell from their demeanor that something serious was afoot.

"Get the warden!" Sullivan ordered.

Roach reached for his radio. After a brief exchange with a colleague in the administration building, they signaled that the warden was on his way.

Sullivan paced back and forth in the reception room. Riley tried reassuring him.

"Sully, it's probably nothing. You had already checked the employee roster here, remember?"

"Maybe I missed something."

"Even so, one officer can't break a prisoner out of here."

"I hope you're right, Riley."

As they went back and forth, the warden finally appeared. He was in visible distress. His hand went up in a blocking gesture immediately.

"I don't have time, gentlemen; I have a crisis going on right now," he declared, shaking his head.

Sullivan could feel his blood pressure rise.

"Does it involve Wallace?"

"Actually, yes."

"What happened?" Riley jumped in.

"It seems he was poisoned."

Sullivan immediately remembered the article about Officer Hughes.

"Let me guess—was it fentanyl?" Sullivan asked.

"We don't know yet, but I will definitely get to the bottom of it. I've started a full investigation."

"No matter, Warden. We believe your staff has been compromised. Take us to your infirmary right away." Sullivan's tone was serious but controlled.

"You don't understand, Agent Sullivan; the inmate is on his way to a hospital right now."

Sullivan could feel the blood draining from his face. He felt a sudden chill. He looked at Riley and then back at the warden.

"Well, guess what, Warden Underwood."

"What?" he replied, puzzled.

"Inmate Wallace just broke out of prison."

———

From the passenger seat, Alexa watched Sergeant Brissey as he drove the van down the desolate country road. Having checked her watch, she knew they were only three miles from her transfer point. Instinctively, she felt her pistol with her right hand. She knew she would be using it shortly.

Turning to look into the passenger compartment of the van, she could see her brother resting, flanked by Gibson and the nurse. She felt an urge to go back and comfort him. However, she knew that would have to wait until they were in a safe place. Until then she had to stay focused on her current mission. She simply had to hope that the nurse was competent.

The nurse had not entered into Alexa's planning. As she thought about this, she felt her presence could be a blessing. Much like Sutter, she could be an invaluable asset. In preparation for the operation, Alexa had spent several hours researching treatments for fentanyl and heroin overdoses. Such treatment primarily focused on hydration, oxygenation, and rest. While well intentioned in her research, she realized Michael's prospects for recovery were much higher with the care of a licensed nurse.

Alexa started to recognize some markers she had memorized along the route. They were almost there. She could feel her pulse quicken. She checked the time for confirmation.

It was 1:03 p.m.

For a moment, the warden felt the room spinning.

"What are you talking about?" he asked.

"Did you recently have a new female officer transfer here?"

"Yes, Amanda Fisher."

"From the East Coast, right?"

"From our headquarters, yes. How did you know that?" Underwood was feeling overwhelmed.

"We just learned that the coyote—posing as your Officer Fisher—is working for the Bureau of Prisons."

"Oh my God." He stammered, thinking. "I have calls to make."

"You need to access her file," Riley jumped in.

"I can do that."

"Not now," Sullivan said. "Let's get on the road."

The warden froze, suddenly hesitant. He was in unchartered waters. He considered that he was an administrator and not a trained fugitive hunter. Yet he also knew that the confinement of Michael Wallace had been his responsibility. By that measure he was a failure. Finally, he made his decision.

"All right, let's go."

As he walked out of the reception area, he grabbed Officer Roach's radio and walked into the light of day. He checked his cell phone, which he now had on his hip.

The time on the screen flashed 1:10 p.m.

———

As Sergeant Brissey drove the transport van, he was in no particular hurry. He had been ordered to take Inmate Wallace to the hospital, and he followed orders. However, he was not told how fast to get there. As far as he was concerned, Wallace could die. He knew full well the horrific crimes for which Wallace was imprisoned.

His wandering mind was disturbed by a movement. Out of the corner of his right eye, Sergeant Brissey felt something was not right. He looked over to Alexa, and his jaw dropped.

The barrel of Alexa's pistol was pointing straight at him.

"Pull over," she said in a low voice, not wanting to alert their passengers.

"What are you doing, Amanda?" he said, raising his voice.

"Pull over now," she demanded, pointing to her secret spot on the side of the road.

As he slowed down and pulled over, he looked over at her again.

"Are you crazy?"

"Over there, closer to the woods," she instructed.

He finally stopped the van where she ordered.

From the rear Officer Gibson yelled out, "Is there a problem up there?"

"Just a mechanical issue. I will be back in a minute!" she yelled back.

"What do you want?" Sergeant Brissey asked, a puzzled look on his face.

"I have what I want, Sarge."

She pointed the gun at his head and fired one round. The bullet went through his skull, and part of his brain and cranium spattered on the dashboard. She had angled the shot to avoid being sprayed herself.

Alexa quickly went to the rear of the van, gun drawn and pointed at Gibson. His face displayed a mix of fear and confusion.

"Drop your gun on the floor!" she ordered, pointing her weapon at him.

Nurse Salter's eyes widened like saucers. She sat next to her unconscious patient, unsure what was happening.

As ordered Gibson slowly put his weapon on the floor.

"What do you want, Fisher?" he asked, thinking the same thing as the sergeant.

"We are transferring him to another vehicle."

"Are you insane?"

"You heard me."

Alexa checked her timepiece.

It was 1:12 p.m.

———

As Sullivan's Impala barreled down the open road, Riley sat quietly in the passenger seat. The warden was in the back, his phone at his ear. He was calling Captain Benham, his most trusted officer, who had already heard there was a situation.

"Benham, call the state police!" he ordered. "Tell them about the van, and have them place roadblocks in a twenty-mile radius around the prison!"

Sullivan listened to the warden over the roar of his engine as he drove, again his accelerator at maximum.

"And have them put out an alert on Officer Amanda Fisher's car, now!"

Sullivan leaned back to speak to the warden, one eye on the road ahead. He had spied the warden's radio as they left the facility.

"Isn't it routine to radio a transport van, to check on their status?" he asked.

"Sure," he answered.

Sullivan looked over at Riley, who had been thinking the same thing.

Back at the Supermax, Captain Benham hung up with the warden and tracked down Alexa's personnel folder. He then dutifully rang the state police.

None of them could have known that those roadblocks would be much farther away than Alexa planned to travel.

———

Colorado State Trooper William Gallagher sat in his patrol car, having just finished writing a traffic report on his silver police laptop. He was parked in a small abandoned parking lot of a defunct gas station on Route 50, between the town of Pueblo West and Florence, when an alert on his laptop rang out.

He checked the screen.

The **BOLO** alarm flashed a picture of Amanda Fisher from her Colorado driver's license and a description of her vehicle, a blue Ford F-150 pickup truck, Colorado license plate BCX1176, with a warning.

> **Be on the lookout.** *Amanda Fisher is believed to be FBI top-ten fugitive Alexa Wallace. Fisher, a.k.a. Wallace, is an officer in the Bureau of Prisons, wearing a prison uniform. She was last seen in a BOP transport van leaving the ADX Supermax in Florence with Inmate Michael Wallace, two other BOP officers, and a nurse. She is armed and extremely dangerous. Do not approach without backup.*

Gallagher could not believe his eyes. A prison escape from the Supermax was unthinkable. In remote Colorado he could never have imagined such a big case. He read the report again for confirmation.

He radioed his intentions. "Two-Nineteen responding to BOLO, headed Route 50 west."

The dispatcher's response was instantaneous. "HQ copies that, Two-Nineteen. Thirteen-twenty hours."

He pulled his cruiser into drive and gunned the engine, headed west toward Florence.

Having placed Michael Wallace, on his stretcher, into the back of Alexa's pickup truck, Gibson and Salter were winded. Salter, in particular, was short of breath, being of slight build. Alexa had offered no assistance as she ordered them quickly, efficiently, into doing her bidding.

The truck was in the woods exactly as Alexa had left it. They were not visible from the road. The van, however, although parked discreetly against the gap in the woods, was visible to an observant passerby. She knew there was little time to spare.

When they were done, Gibson stood before her, his radio still attached to his work belt. He put his arms up to her in a pleading gesture.

"What now?" He said.

Without hesitation, Alexa shot him twice in the chest. He fell back onto a pile of leaves, grass, and twigs. Salter jumped in fear when the shots pierced their quiet wooded sanctuary. Her thoughts turned to her children. Would she ever see them again, she wondered, the fright visible on her face.

"Are you going to kill me?" Salter said.

Alexa stared her down hard, pointing her weapon at her face. "If he dies, you die."

Trembling, Salter shook her head in agreement.

"Get in the back—we've got to go," Alexa ordered.

Once in the truck, Alexa covered Salter and Michael with the plastic tarp. She then warned the nurse one more time: "No tricks. I'll be watching."

As she opened the driver's side door to her truck, she stopped cold when the radio at her hip came alive.

"Transport Van Twenty-Two, status check please."

Alexa's first instinct was to radio back that all was well. However, she had a faint hint of voice recognition. As she replayed the voice in her mind, she realized it was the warden calling.

A radio check to a transport van was normal. Such a check from the warden was not. She realized her identity was now revealed. She ignored the call, knowing that a radio burst could be triangulated, and her position could be vectored.

She knew that the government could remotely turn on a person's cell phone and then use GPS tracking to locate it. For that reason she threw her cell phone on the ground. She knew that Dave Sutter would be tracked down in short order, and he had that number. Her radio, however, could only be tracked if it was transmitting. The radio she kept, to continue monitoring.

Alexa pulled her truck out of the opening and looked down the road, checking both directions. She waited as one sedan passed by and then pulled out onto the road and headed east. She took one last look at the transport van through her side mirror as she drove off.

She checked her watch again, making mental calculations. It was 1:20 p.m.

Her senses were on full alert. She was being hunted.

FORTY ONE

The Hunt

The warden made two more futile attempts to communicate with the transport van. Each failed attempt made him feel sick to his stomach. He was realizing the worst fears of any warden, let alone the chief administrator of a Supermax facility. He dreaded making the call to headquarters in Washington, DC, yet he knew it was inevitable. He looked at his phone as he had this thought. The time flashed 1:21 p.m.

"No response!" he yelled to the front.

He saw Sullivan and Riley look at each other. He could see they had reached a conclusion, but he was puzzled.

"What does that tell us?" He leaned over to them.

"I'm sorry, Warden. It means she's killed your other officers."

"But how?"

"If she was still in cover, either she or one of the other officers would have answered. This means she's revealed herself."

The warden started to feel nauseated. He was about to ask them to pull over when Riley yelled out.

"There!" He pointed.

Having spotted the white BOP van next to the woods, Sullivan hit the brakes hard. Five hundred yards away and outside their range of view, Alexa's pickup truck had just crested the hill in front of them.

Given their high speed, the Impala overshot the van by a few feet, but it mattered not. They pulled over and got out, guns drawn.

"Stay here!" Riley ordered.

Sullivan approached the van from the right, Riley from the left. Immediately, they could see blood on the windshield. They opened the van and found Sergeant Brissey's body in the front. Otherwise, the van was empty.

"There's a path," Sullivan said.

"I see it," Riley answered.

Following the pickup's tire tracks, they walked ten feet apart, slowly, guns at the ready. Finally, they found young Officer Gibson dead on the cold ground. His gun and radio were still on his belt.

They holstered their weapons in disgust.

"Fuck!" Riley yelled.

Sullivan put a hand on his shoulder. "It's all right, Riley."

"Yeah, I know, Sully. We have her now."

Trooper Gallagher had pushed his cruiser westbound to a speed of 110 miles per hour. His blue emergency lights were flashing, clearing his path on the rural road. As an occasional car came toward him, he quickly assessed each vehicle, looking for the prison van or the fugitive's pickup truck. From his experience working the highways over the prior five years, he could quickly determine a car's make and model.

Heading east, in the Trooper's direction, Alexa drove the speed limit of fifty-five miles per hour. In the distance she could see the flash of a cruiser's lights approaching. She knew this might happen before reaching her safe house. Pulling over, she knew, would certainly attract attention and give her away. She thought about how her father counseled that the smallest detail could be the difference between a mission's success or failure. Now, she had to trust that he was right.

As Gallagher's cruiser closed in on Alexa, he slowed down. He could see the vehicle was a Ford pickup truck. Alexa looked forward, her left hand on the steering wheel, her right hand on her holster. As he slowed to sixty miles per hour, he could see the truck was red. He was looking for a blue truck.

He gunned his engine again, continuing westbound.

Alexa silently thanked her father and sped up. She was now only two minutes from the Barrett residence, and safety. She was certain she could not be tracked there.

When Sullivan and Riley returned to the Impala, Warden Underwood was pacing next to the vehicle. From where he was standing, he could see the blood inside the van. To his credit he had stayed put as instructed.

Sullivan spoke first. "I'm sorry, Warden, both officers are dead, and Alexa Wallace is gone."

"Oh my God."

The warden looked like he was having a nervous breakdown. He had turned pale as a sheet.

"What about the nurse?"

"A nurse?" Sullivan said, surprised.

"Yes, I sent our nurse with them. Jo-Ann Salter."

He paused for a moment, considering the implications.

"She's gone, too. She's been taken hostage."

"This can't be happening. Now I have an escaped prisoner *and* a hostage." The warden leaned against the car, a hand to his head.

As Sullivan and Underwood talked, Riley had opened the trunk of the Impala. He was sifting through their bags, looking for one of his electronic tablets. After finding what he was looking for, Riley turned on the device. The tablet was powering up when Sullivan noticed a state police cruiser approaching at maximum speed.

"Looks like we have company," he said.

When Trooper Gallagher pulled over, he immediately recognized the warden. He got out of his cruiser, and he and the warden exchanged a muted, somber greeting.

As they talked, Sullivan conferred with Riley.

"Well?"

"I need a minute. I have to run the program."

As they chatted, waiting for the computer to come into play, they could see that the warden had received a call. As impossible as it seemed, the call was further agitating Underwood. He kept repeating the words "*Yes, sir,*" over and over again. It was clear the call was from someone in authority. Of concern to Sullivan and Riley was the fact that he kept looking over at them as he listened to the phone. When he finally hung up, he walked over to them. Trooper Gallagher followed close behind.

"That was my superior at headquarters. I've been told of your suspensions."

Trooper Gallagher looked on, interested in the drama.

"So what," Sullivan answered.

"So I'm not to have any further interaction with you, period," he said flatly.

"I'm just trying to help you."

"Well, your help is not wanted or needed."

"Suit yourself."

"Further, I'm told the FBI is preparing arrest warrants for the two of you." The warden looked over at Trooper Gallagher.

"Don't look at me, Warden. That's a federal matter," Gallagher interjected.

"You should detain them until the FBI arrives."

Sullivan could not suppress a smile, shaking his head as he watched them. Riley was busy with his tablet, unconcerned.

"I'm sorry, Warden. I don't have a warrant for them."

"Warden, don't you have enough to worry about?" Riley finally jumped in.

Underwood seemed undeterred in pursuing the issue. It was his way of blocking out the more important matters swirling around him that would likely derail his career. The new information gave him a scapegoat.

"Well, Trooper, you need to hold them here."

"That's not happening, Warden. I'm sorry."

Sullivan looked over at Riley. They both had the same thought. They should leave immediately. Soon the scene would be crawling with dozens of federal and local law-enforcement officers. They might not be as sympathetic as Trooper Gallagher. He addressed the warden one final time.

"We're leaving. Good luck. You're going to need it."

Sullivan and Riley jumped in the Impala. In the passenger seat, Riley cradled his tablet, which he quickly plugged into the power outlet. It was now fully lit.

As they pulled away, a state police helicopter roared over them. A moment later another followed. Reinforcements were charging in.

Riley looked back as they drove off.

"I guess he doesn't want to know how we can track them."

Sullivan smiled at his resourceful friend.

———

Jeremiah Barrett had spent two days clearing out the family barn. Years of abandonment had left it littered with junk. By the time he finished, it looked almost new. The Barrett family's new benefactor had told them she would be back in three days with the truck. So on the third day, the Barretts spent the day looking out their living-room window. They had already purchased a new coffee maker with the money Alexa had given them. In their mind that would be the first of many more additions to the home if luck was with them.

As the clock on their kitchen wall struck 1:36 p.m., Barbara Barrett saw the truck first.

"There she is." She pointed down the driveway.

"Go on," she ordered.

On cue, Mr. Barrett walked out and over to the barn.

Alexa smiled as she saw the old man pulling the barn doors open. He had turned out to be reliable. She had already heard one helicopter overhead, so she knew her timing could not be better. She needed shelter quickly.

Once parked in the barn, with the doors closed, Alexa got out and pulled the tarp off the bed of the truck. Mr. Barrett gasped at the sight. Nurse Salter was sweating nervously, despite the cool spring air. She was too nervous to say anything. Her brother was still unconscious.

"What is this?" he asked.

"We have a medical emergency. Help us get him inside."

"This isn't a hospital," he stammered.

"Mr. Barrett"—she looked at him sternly—"you will be compensated."

"Oh, I see."

"And it's police business."

"All right, I guess. I don't know what Barbara will say though."

"I will talk to her."

Alexa motioned to the nurse, who grabbed one side of the stretcher. Alexa grabbed the other end. They carried him off the truck and onto the ground.

"When I say, open the door and let us out."

"OK."

Alexa quickly went to the door and peeked out, looking for any police helicopters or planes. She saw none.

"All right, now!" she ordered.

When Mr. Barrett opened the door, Alexa and Salter wheeled the stretcher across the grass, and then they lifted him up the steps onto the porch. Mrs. Barrett had opened the front door, and Alexa barged in first with her end of the stretcher. Once Nurse Salter was inside, Mr. Barrett followed.

"What is going on here?" Mrs. Barrett bellowed.

Alexa pulled her pistol and smacked her across the side of the head with it. Mrs. Barrett fell back onto the floor. A small cut on her head bled slightly. Mr. Barrett's eyes widened angrily. She could see he was about to charge her. Alexa cut him off, pointing her gun at his head.

"No more questions! I give the orders from now on."

Alexa had already determined that watching three hostages would be impossible. Even two would be difficult. For now, however, she needed the nurse and Mrs. Barrett. Once Mrs. Barrett had composed herself and lifted herself up, Alexa decided to set the tone.

"Mrs. Barrett."

"What do you want?" she answered angrily.

"I want you to pay attention."

Alexa pointed her pistol at her husband. Without another word, she pulled the trigger. The round hit him in the chest in the center of his heart. Mr. Barrett was dead before he hit the ground.

———

Sullivan was driving with one eye on the road, another on Riley. He was careful not to exceed the speed limit. Not for fear of being pulled over. He knew the state police had too much on their hands for traffic enforcement at the moment. His concern was for Riley's task at hand.

He finally looked over.

"Anything?"

"Not yet—keep going."

At that moment, Sullivan felt his phone vibrating in his pocket. He reached down to retrieve it. Immediately, he could see it was his friend and contact in the Denver office.

"Hey there, Banks. I was just about to call you."

"So you know about the warrants?"

"That's not why I was going to call you. I already heard about the warrants."

"Are you crazy, Sully?"

"What do you mean?"

"I mean the FBI is gearing to take you down for interference in the case! This SSA Walker in headquarters went ballistic when he heard what you were doing."

"He has his agenda; I have mine." Sullivan's focus was single-minded.

"Well, I've done all I can, Sully. I just wanted to warn you."

Riley punched Sullivan in the arm with his free hand and then pointed to his screen. *I've got a signal,* he mouthed.

"I was going to call you because we can track the fugitive. I was counting on you to bring the cavalry."

"Sorry, Sully, you're on your own."

Sullivan looked at Riley's screen closely. One icon displayed their vehicle moving eastbound. Another icon displayed a flashing red dot. The dot was getting closer.

"Understood, Banks," he said. "No hard feelings."

He hung up the phone and put his hand on Riley's shoulder. His face radiated an odd combination of resignation and excitement.

"Riley, it's just us. Are you still in?"

"We've come this far."

"All right then. Let's finish this."

———

FORTY TWO

Cavalry

Having driven by the Barrett's residence twice, Riley was certain he had located their prey. He wanted to drive by once more, out of an abundance of caution, but they knew it would not be prudent. If they were being watched from the residence, a third pass by would stick out. Although the road was quite a distance from the residence, they had to assume their fugitive was using binoculars.

Sullivan had pulled over a half mile from the residence. As they sat there for a moment, several police vehicles passed them by, their emergency lights indicating that a full statewide manhunt was underway. As stoically as he had seemed to take the news that he and Riley were persona non grata, he was fuming internally.

He knew he had to shut those feelings down if they were to achieve their goal. This was their last chance. As he had observed the Barrett residence, Sullivan had seen the mountains behind the house. Once Michael Wallace was well enough, he was certain that they would flee to those hills, most likely never to be seen again. He could not take that chance. They had to act soon.

Sullivan leaned over to Riley, who seemed mesmerized by his tablet. "How sure are you?"

Riley frowned. He was mildly annoyed at being questioned in his area of expertise.

"The signal is within five hundred yards of our location, and I don't see anything else within that range. Do you?"

"I guess not, Riley. Sorry."

"The house is perfect for her needs. Did you see the barn?"

"Yes, for her vehicle," Sullivan said.

"So what's the plan?"

"Did you bring any of your toys?" Sullivan smiled.

"Why, yes, I did, Sully."

"Good, then we will wait for darkness. And then hope they fall asleep."

"So there won't be a cavalry charging over the hills to help us?" Riley grinned.

Sullivan reached for his phone. "Maybe there will be."

As they spoke, a swirling vortex of clouds and wind began to slowly descend on their valley. It was still too far for them to hear the lightning and thunder claps, although the national weather service was monitoring the cold front. They would soon be issuing a storm warning.

———

Having delivered her deadly message, Alexa quickly and decisively set the tone inside the Barrett residence. Both of her hostages became instantly compliant.

Alexa quickly scoured the residence for any threats. She first went to the kitchen, in the rear of the house. She found some sharp kitchen knives and threw them out the back door and into a set of bushes. She then locked the rear door, flipping the dead bolt into place.

She then turned her attention to her brother's needs.

Although putting Michael in the master bedroom would give him the most comfort, Alexa knew she needed a central place to keep a watch on her hostages. She needed to create a command center. So with the help of Nurse Salter and Mrs. Barrett, they placed her brother on the living-room couch, his head propped with a pillow, a blanket over his body.

Salter took Michael's pulse and quickly set up a new IV line. Alexa watched her from the hallway, where, using a knife, she cut the telephone cord into the residence. She turned on the television, and a photo of Amanda Fisher, in uniform, flashed on the screen. The scroll under the image announced that a manhunt was underway for her and her brother. This was not news to Alexa.

A news crew was at the bloody scene where she had left the van. The camera panned to a news reporter on the scene, behind yellow crime-scene tape. Alexa grabbed the remote and muted the sound. There was nothing she could learn from what he was currently reporting. She finally went to her brother's side.

Alexa put a hand on his head, gently.

"How is he?"

"His pulse is weak, but he is stable. He should make it."

"I will hold you to that," she scowled.

"I should get some moist towels."

"No," Alexa said firmly. "Stay with him."

She turned to Mrs. Barrett. "You heard her. Take me to your bathroom."

"Sure," she replied.

As they walked down the hall to the bathroom, Barbara Barrett looked about for anything she could use as a weapon. Despite her age, she was not used to being told what to do, let alone in her own home. A slow rage was boiling inside her. If she got the chance, she thought to herself, she would teach this young woman a lesson.

—

Having achieved his breakthrough with Detective Dominguez, Conrad had taken the first flight to Washington, DC. He had hoped that headquarters would have a change of heart in light of recent events. Once he heard from Sullivan that they were able to track their fugitive, he was certain they would listen. Having no FBI credentials, he waited in the lobby at FBI HQ for an audience with SSA Bill Walker.

Once Wallace's escape was reported, FBI HQ had activated a crisis action team at its Strategic Information and Operations Center (SIOC). The SIOC was a twenty-four-hour operations center, capable of handling several major crises at once. SSA Walker was at the helm of the table, coordinating information as it came in. He had already placed the Denver SWAT team on alert. When he got news that Conrad was waiting for a meeting, he ignored it. However, an hour later, another agent tapped Walker on the shoulder and counseled him to at least meet with Conrad.

Walker waited another hour before finally making his way to the lobby. The irritation was written on his face like an electronic billboard.

"What is it, Mr. Conrad?"

"We need help in Colorado. We have a way to track the fugitives."

"Bullshit."

"I'm telling you—"

"You're lucky we don't have a warrant for *you*, Mr. Conrad," he interrupted.

"We can track them—"

"Impossible. I'm sick of your and Sullivan's supposed magic tricks."

"You won't listen?"

"No. Further, I'm asking you to leave right now."

Conrad, shaking his head, headed for the exit in disgust. He only had one play left. He could not let his friends twist in the wind.

Alexa used a moist hand towel to gently wipe the sweat from her brother's forehead. The nurse, next to her, watched her as she did so. From the corner love seat, Mrs. Barrett kept a close eye on them. Occasionally, she would turn her attention to the muted television report. Alexa did the same, with an eye to seeing if anything appeared to indicate danger. At the moment, the news crews were filming a pair of tracking dogs called to help in the hunt. She knew that technique would be useless to them in their search.

Salter monitored Inmate Wallace's condition with growing concern. It was not Alexa's warning that had her worried. It was the growing prospect that in her professional opinion, Michael Wallace would survive. She had seen the ruthlessness of her captor. Once she was of no use, she feared, Alexa would surely kill her.

"This is your brother, right?" she asked softly.

"Yes."

"I can see you love him very much."

"Don't bother with chitchat. Just do your job."

Alexa got up and walked to the window, pulling the curtain aside and looking toward the road. She saw a car pass by in the distance but nothing out of the ordinary. She turned to Mrs. Barrett, who sat silently on the love seat.

"Don't think you are just going to sit here all day."

Mrs. Barrett stared back, hard. Behind Alexa she could see the closet door where her husband had been stuffed. Alexa had not even bothered to place him there gently. She had pushed and twisted him brusquely, squeezing him in. Mrs. Barrett's husband of forty years had been disposed of in a few twisted moments.

Alexa pointed her gun at her and then waved it toward the kitchen.

"Your job is to feed us. Get busy."

—

The afternoon sun was shining brightly on the gray tarmac at the Capitol Area Helo Tours compound. Retired Captain Jim McDougal, having already received a call, was waiting outside his office when Jimmy Conrad pulled into the business. Following Conrad were McDougal's new partners, Jorge and Miguel, who quickly parked their car and jumped out to greet Conrad.

Conrad was in no mood for small talk.

"Mr. McDougal, we need your help once more."

"Yes, Jorge briefed me." McDougal looked at him sternly, his sunglasses bouncing the light off his face.

"What's your fastest chopper?"

Miguel and Jorge had already tried to talk Conrad out of a helicopter. They had warned him that helicopters were not meant for a long flight like the one he had in mind. It was preferable to take a plane. However, he was undeterred.

"A plane would be quicker," McDougal answered.

"They've already pitched that idea," Conrad replied, looking at his friends.

"But there's no airport where I'm going."

McDougal looked over at his newly acquired Sikorsky S-92 helicopter. It was a prototype and his most expensive aircraft.

Conrad followed his gaze and started looking over at the dark-green chopper. As he did so, McDougal sized him up, guessing his weight at around two hundred pounds. He then retrieved a small tablet and started making calculations on it with a stylus. Estimating mileage combined with payload weight, airspeed, and refueling, he scribbled furiously. Finally, he looked up.

"On my faster helicopter, *if* you are the only passenger, it will take you at least six hours, with one refueling stop."

"That's the best you can do?"

"Yes, and that's assuming no inclement weather."

"Understood," he said looking at the brothers. "One of you will have to stay behind."

———

Three quarters of a mile north of the Barrett residence, Sullivan found a safe clearing to park his car discreetly. Given the circumstances, it was the best command center they could muster. While he considered their plan of action, Riley was hunched over the trunk, checking his equipment before it got dark.

A line of sinister, threatening clouds had started to move in. They had already heard the storm warning over the radio. The forecast called for a fast-moving system. Typically, those were the most damaging storms, he knew. However, given the situation, he thought the bad weather could be used as a cover for their advance.

His windshield started to receive an incoming drizzle, when his phone buzzed. He picked up immediately.

"Sully!" Conrad yelled over the noise of the helicopter. "I'm on my way."

"I'm not sure I can wait, Jimmy," he yelled back.

"Wait for me!" he yelled louder.

"I have to go in there in a few hours. I can't wait until morning."

"Wait!" he pleaded.

"Well, hurry up!"

"I'm going as fast as I can!"

"Riley will send you our coordinates."

Conrad hung up the line and turned to Jorge, who was piloting the chopper. He was the natural choice for the mission as he was the smaller of the two brothers.

"Faster, Jorge!"

As he looked west, Conrad could see the sun, drenched in orange, hanging low and descending into the horizon.

FORTY THREE

Darkness

Large raindrops pelted the Barrett residence, which inside the home sounded like popcorn in a microwave oven. The wind rattled the windows of the old wooden house. Alexa had given up looking out the window. There was nothing to see. An eerie darkness had enveloped the home like a black bag placed over a hostage's head.

Alexa sat on the floor next to the couch. She held Michael's hand, warily watching Mrs. Barrett, who had assumed her position on the love seat. Alexa felt the old lady was a potential threat, despite her age. She had fed them without incident, to be sure, but Alexa felt her usefulness might be coming to an end, soon.

The nurse had placed a chair at the head of the couch, from where she monitored her patient.

Alexa had turned on the TV's volume in anticipation of the eleven o'clock news. Several hours had elapsed. Perhaps the news would shed information of value. A news reporter had been allowed into a command tent erected near one of the many roadblocks the police had set up. He had the demeanor of someone reporting from a war front.

"As you can see, roadblocks have been set up throughout Fremont County. Still, there have been no credible sightings. Police and FBI agents will start door-to-door canvassing in the morning, once this storm has passed."

Again, her picture was broadcast on the TV screen, this time accompanied by a prison photo of her brother. A hot-line number was placed on the scroll under the photos. *A door-to-door canvass*, she thought. That was not a good scenario.

The station then turned to a commercial. Alexa got up and turned the volume down. As she did, she heard a gargling sound. Her brother was stirring.

"He's waking!" Salter called out.

Michael's first act after regaining partial consciousness was to vomit. The nurse quickly leaned him to his side, and soaked it with a towel.

"What's happening?" Alexa demanded.

"This is good. He's purging his system."

Michael's eyes opened slightly. He squinted, looking about, disoriented.

"Just relax, Michael," Alexa said soothingly. "You're going to be all right."

He clutched her hand tightly and leaned his head back onto his pillow. A minute later he had fallen asleep again.

—

Having refueled at a small airport outside of Lincoln, Nebraska, Jorge had once again lifted the chopper rapidly off the ground. At Conrad's insistence he kept the helicopter at a low altitude. Conrad looked back to the lights in Lincoln and then to the darkness as they headed west over the vast Nebraska plain.

The whirring blades blocked out all sound as the engine revved to its maximum capacity. The countryside passed beneath them faster than a bullet train.

In his dark yet fast-moving solitude, Conrad thought back to his last talk with Sullivan. He could tell from his voice that he had no intention of waiting.

Faster, faster, he thought.

—

As midnight approached, almost twelve hours after he was poisoned, Michael stirred again. Alexa was by his side as he did. Mrs. Barrett and the nurse had fallen asleep from exhaustion.

This time, Michael had regained more of his senses. He smiled tightly and squeezed her hand. Alexa went to the kitchen and brought back a glass of water. She lifted his head and poured some for him, which he gladly swallowed. His mouth felt like cotton.

"How long?" he whispered.

"Almost twelve hours."

He shook his head slowly, wincing. "You poisoned me. Was that your best plan?"

She smiled. "It worked, didn't it?"

He patted her hand and nodded his head.

"Go back to sleep," she said. "You need your rest."

As he leaned back into his pillow, Alexa knew that if the police were going to canvass the county, he would indeed need his rest.

———

Sullivan and Riley waited until the storm was in full force. Then, once the sky was alive with flashing light and the thunder was its chorus, they moved in. Following a tall tree line, they walked down from the road and along the side of the residence. The windows along their side of the house were dark. Clearly, nobody was in those rooms. Through a slit in the front curtain, however, they had seen light emanating from what they assumed was a living room. On that basis they crept to the back of the home.

Using his lock-picking tools and under the cover of the pelting rain and rocking thunder, Riley began to work on the rear kitchen door.

Once it was unlocked, he pulled the door open a crack. On cue Sullivan then placed a small rubber ball through the door. Riley then gently shut the door tight.

———

When Michael stirred again, he was clearly out of the woods. The nurse, awoken by Alexa, took his pulse. She gave a silent thumbs-up after releasing the pressure from the cardio cuff. Under his own power, he lifted himself into a semiseated position on the couch.

"Where are we?" he finally asked softly.

"I found a house near the prison."

"That's smart. I'm sure there are roadblocks. We wouldn't get far."

"We will have to hike it from here. I have some gear."

"I would hike Mount Everest if it meant freedom, my little sister." He lovingly put a hand on her face.

"Before I forget," she said, handing him her service pistol. Her own pistol she kept at her waist.

"I will keep this close," he said, eyeing Mrs. Barrett, who snored gently on the love seat.

The nurse, seeing the pistol, moved her chair back slightly. She did not want them to think she was eavesdropping.

"I have so much to tell you."

"I knew you would come through for me. I just knew." He gushed.

"Michael, we aren't alone."

"What do you mean?"

"Father left us a note at our rendezvous point."

"What did it say?"

"It was a code with numbers."

"Which you cracked." He smiled.

"Yes, it's a set of coordinates."

As they spoke, a loud thunderclap shook the house. Mrs. Barrett stirred. Squinting, she looked down at the floor. She thought she could see a mouse under the TV stand. It would not be the first mouse, she thought.

"Did you track it down?"

"No, I wanted us to go together."

"Where is it?"

"It's a remote island in Northern Maine. It's on a lake."

"That sounds like another Fortress," he whispered.

"Yes. That's what I thought."

Mrs. Barrett saw the movement again. She put on her glasses and looked harder. This time, she could see it was not a mouse. It was a ball of some sort. She quickly realized its purpose and stopped looking at it, not wanting to give it away. Her heart started pounding.

From their perch outside the kitchen, Riley and Sullivan watched the screen on Riley's tablet. The mobile rubber robot had four cameras embedded in it. No matter where it rested, one camera could monitor the action. With his finger Riley moved his hand along the screen, piloting the robot.

In a few short minutes, the ball had toured the entire first floor of the house. A door leading to the basement was quickly noted. Riley pointed to the image, his finger jutting downward. Sullivan understood. Riley would head to the basement and cut the power.

Now, the robot had Alexa and Michael under observation.

"I once overheard our parents talking about us having cousins."

"That must be them!" Alexa said excitedly.

With the next thunderclap, Riley opened the door again, and they both quietly slipped inside.

"Is that where we are headed then?"

"Where else? We can start again, with our cousins."

"That's going to be some hike," he joked quietly.

Riley made his way to the basement and in short order found the circuit board.

Sullivan waited in the kitchen. With the robot's help, he had mapped the house in his head. He knew the layout. He was only steps away from the living room and his distracted fugitives. He was drenched, drops of water falling onto the floor. He hoped they could not hear that over the storm.

"We can make it. I know we can," she continued.

"When do we leave?"

"At dawn."

"I hope I can keep up with you."

"I'm sure you can. You were always the strongest." She reached for his hand.

In that moment, she felt his watch. She had not noticed it before. "What's this?"

"My watch. They let me have it," he said, suddenly concerned by her reaction.

"Who gave it to you?" Alexa stood up in her seat next to him.

"In the prison the FBI gave it to me. To try and bribe me."

At that moment, she thought she heard someone in the house.

"Oh no, Michael!" She gasped.

Suddenly, another bolt of lightning struck the ground nearby, shaking the foundation, and the house went dark.

Sullivan ran toward Alexa, who could not see him, but who heard his approach. She reached for her pistol. As she did so, Mrs. Barrett bashed her on the head from behind with the TV remote control. Alexa swung around and kicked her in the chest, knocking her back. When she turned around again, Sullivan was already there.

He punched her directly in the nose, breaking it. She fell back, bloodied but defiantly reaching for her weapon. Sullivan put his gun to her left eye, and she froze.

"You won't kill me, Agent Sullivan," she hissed.

"Watch me," he answered, pulling the trigger. The hollow-point round tore a tunnel through her face and brain.

In a panic Mrs. Barrett got up and ran out the front door, leaving it open in her wake. The open door allowed the lightning to momentarily illuminate the living room.

Nurse Salter saw Michael pointing his weapon, and she screamed. "Watch out!"

Sullivan turned his focus to Michael. He saw the muzzle flash and then felt a pain in his chest. At first it felt like a pinprick. Then he knew. He had been shot.

In his weakened state, Michael's grip was not firm enough for the gun to rack another round properly. He pulled the trigger again, but it would not shoot.

Sullivan walked over to Michael and grabbed the gun out of his hands. He threw it out the open front door. He then placed the muzzle of his gun against Michael's forehead.

"Go ahead. Do it!" Michael screamed.

Sullivan could feel himself losing consciousness. He was light-headed. With his last ounce of strength, he cracked Michael's skull with the butt of his gun.

He collapsed onto the floor, immobilized. In seconds Riley ran up from the basement and reached his side.

As Sullivan drifted into unconsciousness, the last thing he heard was not a boom from the heavens. Nor was it a choir of angels. It was the whirring blade of a helicopter.

FORTY FOUR

TWO DAYS LATER

Light

Sullivan breathed quietly through a ventilator in the intensive-care unit. He remained unconscious, having been placed in a medically induced coma. The doctors at Colorado Springs Memorial Medical Center were among the best in the state. The medical center was a level-one trauma center with the best equipment and staff. As sympathetic as they were to Sullivan's friends, they had said little to the team. Technically, none of them constituted his "family."

A team of doctors took turns checking on his condition. The hospital staff was still abuzz over the excitement of what had occurred two days previously.

Nurse Salter enjoyed her small slice of fame. She had given several media interviews about her ordeal as well as the helicopter flight to the hospital. She was quick to point out that it was her suggestion to fly to a level-one trauma center, rather than the closer hospital in Florence. Medical experts interviewed by the press stated that this was most likely why Sullivan was still alive. None, however, would render a prognosis for recovery.

Barbara Barrett was found the next morning, hiding under a large bush. She was treated at the scene but refused admission to a hospital. The media called her a hero for her actions, and she was quite popular on all the major news networks. Donations poured in from around the country to help her pay for her husband's funeral.

Warden Robert Underwood was quietly and unceremoniously reassigned to a position in Washington, DC, never to run another prison. Although he did nothing wrong, he was the first administrator of a Supermax to have a prisoner escape.

David Sutter had been interrogated for twenty-four hours and released. They could find no evidence that he was aware of Alexa's true identity. He was so shaken by what happened, he promised himself to never trust anyone again. He refused all media inquiries.

At the Florence Medical Center, Michael Wallace was recovering from his injuries. His head having been crushed by the blow from Sullivan's gun, he was also in a coma. He was guarded by six heavily armed US marshals. They would take no more chances with him.

———

The team waited in the lobby until they were given a green light to visit their friend, their patience almost exhausted. Once they were finally allowed to the room, they practically stampeded to the elevator.

Conrad walked in the room first, and the first thing he did was pull back the curtain. As he did, the bright sunlight evaporated the shadow that had covered Sullivan's bed. Conrad felt that the light might somehow awaken his friend. It did not.

Conrad and O'Keefe took a seat on one side of the bed. Trish kept a magazine on her lap but couldn't concentrate to read it. She also couldn't stand to watch Sullivan lying helplessly on the bed. She stole an occasional glance only.

Riley sat alone on the other side of the bed. As usual he quietly distracted himself with his phone and tablet.

As they waited for a doctor or nurse to question, they heard a commotion coming from the hallway. To their surprise FBI Director Franklin walked into the room, flanked by his security detail.

"Welcome, Mr. Franklin," Conrad said, standing to greet him. Riley and O'Keefe also stood.

"I'm checking on one of my agents," he said, smiling.

"Does that mean—" O'Keefe asked quietly.

"Yes, Agent Conrad," he said to Jimmy. "I'm reinstating you and your entire Boston team, effectively immediatcly."

"Thank you, sir."

"What is his prognosis?" He looked over at Sullivan's bed.

"We don't know, sir; I overheard a nurse saying he has a fifty-fifty chance."

"I'm sure he'll make it."

"We hope so," Conrad answered.

Franklin then turned to Riley.

"I read your report"

"Yes, sir."

"What made you think to put a tracking chip in his watch?"

"It was our insurance policy."

Franklin immediately thought to himself, *That's funny because your team was my insurance policy.* He thought it best to keep that quiet.

"Well, it sure worked out. Good job." He slapped Riley on the back.

Franklin left as quickly as he had arrived.

For several minutes the group sat silently. The only noise was the chatter in the hallway outside and the sound of Sullivan's ventilator.

The solitude was eventually interrupted by a sound at the door. To their surprise it was Suzanne Goldwein carrying a box.

"Goldwein, glad you could make it." Conrad greeted her.

They all took turns hugging her. She pointed at Sullivan.

"You know he got himself shot just so I couldn't arrest him."

They all laughed out loud.

"What's in the box?" O'Keefe asked.

"Ah," she said, opening it, "champagne and ice."

They all smiled broadly. Conrad shook his head.

"We'll take turns refilling the ice bucket."

"Agreed."

They placed the champagne on the nightstand beside his bed and started their vigil.

EPILOGUE

The shallow lake water shimmered in the bright moonlight of Northern Maine. A minor drought, combined with a low tide, had lowered the depth on one side of the lake to only about a foot. This allowed a small family of coyotes to cross the lake and explore the island in the center. Previous attempts to make the crossing had been unsuccessful. Now that they were across, they hoped to find new sources of food.

The female coyote kept her two pups close to her as they wandered through a trail. In the darkness her senses were on alert. Her nose told her there was food nearby.

Her pups found a pile of dead leaves under a bush to rest in. After they fell asleep, their mother continued exploring.

As she walked through the dense vegetation, her ears suddenly perked up. She could hear a noise in the distance, and voices. She walked forward, crouching down, quietly advancing.

Through a clearing she finally saw what was making the noise. A campfire was burning, surrounded by humans. Behind them were several structures. The coyote knew from experience that humans were rarely dangerous, and their presence always meant food.

She decided she would return after they were sleeping.

The coyote returned to her napping pups. She looked up hungrily at the low moon and howled.

The End

About the Author

Michael C. De La Peña resides in the Boston area. He is a graduate of George Washington University. He has been an FBI agent for over twenty-five years. He is a trained polygraph examiner. Comments or opinions can be addressed to the author at thecoyotewars@gmail.com or at the Coyote Wars Facebook page.

Made in the USA
Middletown, DE
12 September 2015